NONSENSE

NONSENSE

How to Overcome It

Robert J. Gula

STEIN AND DAY/*Publishers*/New York

First published in 1979
Copyright © 1979 by Robert J. Gula
All rights reserved
Designed by David Miller
Printed in the United States of America
Stein and Day/*Publishers*/Scarborough House
Briarcliff Manor, N.Y. 10510

Library of Congress Cataloging in Publication Data

Gula, Robert J
    Nonsense, how to overcome it.

    Includes bibliography and index.
        1. Influence (Psychology) 2. Logic. I. Title.
    BF774.G84   155.9   79-65121
    ISBN 0-8128-2677-9

Contents

Foreword

*"I just know that that doesn't make
any sense, but I'm not sure why."*

It's frustrating to know in your heart that what you've just heard is
nonsense but not to be able to pinpoint why it is nonsense. If you've
ever found yourself in that position, this book should help. It identifies and itemizes the many different guises that erroneous thinking
may assume, and it explains some of the reasons for erroneous
thinking. This book will not turn you into a skilled rebuttalist, but
it will give you the ammunition to become one. And, even more
important, it will put you in a position of strength in steering a
discussion.

You'll find many of your friends and acquaintances throughout
these pages, but you will also find yourself from time to time. None
of us is immune to nonsense.

A Tale

But when I tell him he hates flatterers,
He says he does, being then most flattered.
Shakespeare, *Julius Caesar*, II, i

"Your Majesty, the news is not good. The infantry has been cut off at Lungdau. General Borkesthal lies mortally wounded, dying in agonizing pain. The enemy have taken Loden and Kranstanbul. They hold the villagers hostage—except those whom they have slain. Marles is in flames. The cavalry has been intercepted at Pestalberg and is now in the very moment of surrender. Through only the most fortuitous workings of God and Nature have I managed to escape these tragedies so that I might report to you the events of these previous days."

"So—This is all you can say. This news is unacceptable. Surely you are a traitor. I will not tolerate disloyalty. Guards, take him! Off with his head! Only an evil person brings such evil tidings. Surely such evil invites the wrath of heaven!"

The king's behavior is outrageous—who will disagree? Not liking what he hears, he blames the messenger for the message.

"Thank goodness things like that don't happen anymore," we're tempted to say. "Thank goodness that we are in a reasonable age where bullies and butchers can no longer arbitrarily treat people like that. Sure, an occasional despot will act like the king and transfer his resentment onto some scapegoat. But such occurrences are infrequent and are universally deplored."

Indeed, very few have the power to do what the king did. People are not often executed as was the unfortunate messenger. And the occasional murdering tyrant *is* universally deplored.

But . . . the spirit of that king isn't dead. Many people act with the king's motivation: people who are intolerant of the viewpoints of others; who insist upon hearing only what they want to hear; who refuse to hear what does not conform to their beliefs, attitudes, biases, and prejudices; who judge the speaker by his statements; who become angry with one who expresses a conflicting opinion; who regard a conflicting opinion as a sign of hostility or disloyalty; who make hasty judgments; who don't bother to determine the facts before expressing an opinion; who take personally what is uttered objectively; and who judge an issue not by what a person is saying but from the personality of the speaker.

The king was rash; so are many people. The king became angry with a person who spoke words that the king did not want to hear; many people treat others in a similar fashion. Like the king, many people, when they become frustrated or threatened, lash out against the nearest available party, and that party is often innocent of any guilt. Like the king, many are comfortable only with companions who share their attitudes and beliefs: "A real friend is someone who agrees with me."

The king was guilty of many fallacies in reasoning, among them a circumstantial *ad hominem* argument, an appeal to force, a *non sequitur,* an illicit contrast, a faulty syllogism, a hasty generalization, a false cause and effect relationship, oversimplification, overreacting, equivocation, and rationalization.

The pages that follow will introduce you to these fallacies and a host of others. You'll also see how such fallacies crop up frequently in daily situations. And while the fallacies that we use and meet from day to day rarely have the fatal consequences that the king's did upon the messenger, the results can be serious nevertheless. And even when they're not serious, they can cause anger, frustration, and wasted words, and they can prevent a discussion from ever reaching a reasonable conclusion. We'll also make occasional observations about human nature, for, if human nature were not as capricious as it is, fallacies would have little impact. The two—human nature and the fallacies—work together to remind us of the spirit of the king.

2

On Laws and Principles

*The chess-board is the world; the pieces are the phe-
nomena of the universe; the rules of the game are what
we call the laws of Nature. The player on the other side is
hidden from us. We know that his play is always fair,
just, and patient. But also we know, to our cost, that he
never overlooks a mistake or makes the smallest allowance
for ignorance.*

Thomas Huxley, A *Liberal Education*

The world is full of laws. There are laws of God and of man, laws of
science and of nature, laws of grammar and of linguistics, laws of
music and of architecture, laws of economics and of mathematics,
and finally there are laws of human behavior.

Sometimes these laws are imposed upon man to maintain order
and to protect rights: the Ten Commandments and most civil law,
for instance. Some laws appear as codes: the Hippocratic oath, for
instance, which was designed to maintain a standard of ethics
among physicians. Other laws are merely conventions to preserve
civility: One does not put one's elbows on the dinner table; one
does not express one's sexual interests toward another person without some courtship ritual. The laws of traditional harmony evolved
to avoid an unpleasant or imbalanced sound and to preserve the
relative distinctness of each of the musical voices: the famous in-
junction against parallel octaves and fifths, for instance, which students of harmony meet early in their career.

There are laws that are idealistic: Seward's *Higher Law*—"The
Constitution devotes the domain to union, to justice, to defense, to

welfare, and to liberty. But there is a higher law than the Constitution, which regulates our authority over the domain, and devotes it to the same noble purpose"—or patriotic, such as that of manifest destiny: It is the manifest destiny of the United States "to overspread the continent allotted by Providence for the free development of our yearly multiplying millions"—or generic, such as the phrase "Draconian law," derived from the seventh century B.C. Athenian, Draco, whose laws were known for their severity (almost everything was punishable by death) and were often described as being written in blood, not ink—or retributive: the *lex talionis*, the law of retaliation, an eye for an eye, a tooth for a tooth.

Then there are laws that have been deduced: To every action there is an equal and opposite reaction (Newton's third law of motion); the total equivalent amount of energy plus mass in the universe remains constant (the law of conservation of energy); something will float if its weight exactly equals the weight of the liquid it displaces (Archimedes' principle); at a constant temperature, the pressure of a gas will decrease when a container is made larger and will increase when a container is made smaller (Boyle's law); heat tends to move from a hot place to a cold place (the second law of thermodynamics).

There are Mendel's laws of genetics, Planck's laws of radiation, Galileo's laws of gravity and mechanics, Keppler's laws of planetary motion, and Ohm's laws of electrical current.

These laws are attempts to describe natural phenomena, to observe what appear to be invariable patterns and to identify the components of those patterns.

Similar description occurs with the less precise laws of the social sciences: Gresham's law of economics (Bad money drives out good); Grimm's laws of linguistic sound changes and correspondences; the law of diminishing returns, applicable both to economics and to behavior: There comes a point when your investment in money or time or energy is not effecting a commensurate yield, i.e., you're not getting your money's or your time's or your energy's worth; at that point it's time to stop. And there is the informal law of the stock market: You can be a bull or a bear, but don't be a pig.

These laws, like the laws of science, observe patterns and the effect these patterns have upon phenomena. But since these patterns are not invariable, these laws have a much weaker stamp of authenticity than do the laws of science. Whereas the laws of science are deductive, the laws of the social sciences are inductive and empirical. They deal with common sense rather than with absolutes.

An offshoot of these empirical laws are the laws of human behavior. There is the Peter principle: In a hierarchy, every employee tends to rise to his level of incompetence—and its corollaries: In time, every post tends to be occupied by an employee who is incompetent to carry out its duties; work is accomplished by those employees who have not yet reached their level of incompetence; employees in a hierarchy do not really object to incompetence, but they do object to people who have pull; good followers do not become good leaders; in most hierarchies, employees with the greatest leadership potential cannot become leaders.

There is Parkinson's law: Work expands so as to fill the time available for its completion—and its corollaries: The more time we have, the less we get done; the more we have to do, the more we get done—and axioms: An official wants to multiply subordinates, not rivals; officials make work for each other.

There is Nagle's law: Complex matters are not susceptible to simple solutions—and Aronson's law: People who do crazy things are not necessarily crazy.

And of course there are Murphy's laws: If anything can go wrong, it invariably will; left to themselves, things always go from bad to worse; nothing is ever as simple as it first seems; if there is a possibility of several things going wrong, the one that will go wrong is the one that will do the most damage; everything you decide to do costs more than first estimated; nature always sides with the hidden flaw; every activity takes more time than you have; the second-best guesser is usually the boss—and is always wrong; if you improve or tinker with something long enough, eventually it will break; whatever you set out to do, something else must be done first; by making something absolutely clear, somebody will be confused; you can fool some of the people all of the time, and all of the people some of the time, and that's sufficient; if everything seems to be going well, you have obviously overlooked something.

The intriguing process of deriving general principles from observed phenomena forces one to wonder whether there are any laws that govern human reasoning. All of us have observed public meetings that accomplished nothing, discussions that lost sight of what was being discussed, and dialogues that were crammed with irrelevancies. And we've all read editorials and letters to editors that presented an unfair and often distorted response to a situation. Very few people actually seem to know what they are talking about, even when they are arguing dogmatically. Muddled thinking seems to be the rule, not the exception. Most discussions are characterized by irrelevancy and confusion. There is nonsense everywhere.

Is man by nature a hopelessly muddled creature? By nature, yes. Muddled, yes. Hopelessly, no. Man may be a rational animal, but he is not by nature a reasoning animal. Careful and clear thinking requires a certain rigor; it is a skill, and, like all skills, it requires training, practice, and vigilance. Before one can use one's reason, he should know the traps that are always awaiting the untutored mind. Hence this book—a book on nonsense, a summary of the devices that camouflage and subvert reason. If we recognize the pitfalls and the ruses, we may be able to avoid them and we may be able to discourage others from relying upon them.

First, some general principles. Let's not call them laws; and, since they're not particularly original, I won't attach my name to them. They are merely a description of patterns that seem to characterize the ways that people tend to respond and think.

1. People tend to believe what they want to believe.

2. People tend to project their own biases or experiences upon situations.

3. People tend to generalize from a specific event.

4. People tend to get personally involved in the analysis of an issue and tend to let their feelings overcome a sense of objectivity.

5. People are not good listeners. They hear selectively. They often hear only what they want to hear.

6. People are eager to rationalize.

7. People are often unable to distinguish what is relevant from what is irrelevant.

8. People are easily diverted from the specific issue at hand.

9. People are usually unwilling to explore thoroughly the ramifications of a topic; people tend to oversimplify.

10. People often judge from appearances. They observe something, misinterpret what they observe, and make terrible errors in judgment.

11. People often simply don't know what they are talking about, especially in matters of general discussion. They rarely think carefully before they speak, but they allow their feelings, prejudices, biases, likes, dislikes, hopes, and frustrations to supersede careful thinking.

12. People rarely act according to a set of consistent standards. Rarely do they examine the evidence and then form a conclusion. Rather, they tend to do whatever they want to do and to believe whatever they want to believe and then find whatever evidence will support their actions or their beliefs. They often think selectively: in evaluating a situation they are eager to find reasons to support what they want to support and they are just as eager to ignore or disregard reasons that don't support what they want.

13. People often do not say what they mean and they often do not mean what they say.

To these principles, let's add four observations cited by J. A. C. Brown in his *Techniques of Persuasion:* "Most people want to feel that issues are simple rather than complex, want to have their prejudices confirmed, want to feel that they 'belong' with the implication that others do not, and need to pinpoint an enemy to blame for their frustrations."

The above comments may seem jaundiced. They are not meant to be. They are not even meant to be critical or judgmental. They merely suggest that it is a natural human tendency to be subjective rather than objective and that the untrained mind will usually take the path of least resistance. The path of least resistance is rarely through reason.

Interlude: A Brief History of Nonsense

The best way to come to truth [is] to examine things as really they are, and not to conclude they are as we fancy of ourselves, or have been taught by others to imagine.
Locke, *Essay Concerning Human Understanding,* II, xii

Has reason always been an elusive faculty? History suggests that the answer is yes. As early as the fifth century B.C., Plato identified the problem:

We have both observed many discussions and have noticed that it is not easy for people, discussing their views with another person, to come to an agreement. Rather, when they disagree, one person says that the other person is wrong; then they get angry; then each thinks that the other has a vested interest or that the other is simply a trouble-maker; and each accuses the other of avoiding the issue. Then they finally storm away from each other with insults. Even the bystanders are embarrassed.

· · ·

A person doesn't have to be wise; he doesn't have to know what he is talking about; he merely has to appear to the ignorant to know more than the person who does know what he is talking about.

These paraphrases from the *Gorgias* suggest that people indeed often don't know how to communicate, that their communication often fails, and that, in fact, they are easily fooled.

Aristotle approaches the situation from a slightly different angle. He identifies three improper ways of approaching an audience: "One type of person, not being very able, does not understand the question with sufficient clarity; another type, while he does understand the question, does not speak his mind candidly; a third type, while being both able and honorable, does not have the interest of the audience at heart."

Aristotle comments that the ignorant often have considerable influence over the masses—more so, in fact, than do the knowledgeable—for the ignorant are so much closer to the sentiments and mentality of the masses.

The playwright Euripides in his *Hippolytus* has Theseus comment:

O men who vainly err in so many ways, why do you teach so many thousands of skills and devise and discover so many things when you have not yet learned or even tried to learn to teach the ignorant to use their brains.

The ignorant masses, often well intentioned but usually hopelessly deceived by appearances and invariably eager to persist in their narrow beliefs, appear frequently in classical drama.

Cicero, writing several hundred years later, tells how a person can be persuasive: "The speaker must be liked by the audience; he should be able to move his audience more by the emotions than by reason, for people base their judgments much more on hate or love or desire or anger or sadness or happiness or hope or fear or some other emotion than upon truth or upon law." He later cites ways to win over a judge:

Get them to hate or to like or to envy or to fear or to hope or to desire or to shudder or to be happy or to be sad or to pity or to be indignant; ... a speaker should try to touch feelings in the judge's heart that will lead in favor of the speaker's position. For it is easier, as the saying goes, to get a runner to move faster than to get running someone who is not moving at all. . . . When I take on a new case, I make it a point to find out just what the judge's biases and beliefs are so that I can use the right strategy in winning him over.

It is so much easier to feel than to reason! People are susceptible to the right approach, but the speaker must be careful:

We appeal to the feelings of our audience. We can effect love, for instance, if we can show that what we are saying is advantageous to them; we show that the position we are advocating will add to their prestige or their profit. If we are defending someone, we show that that person has never worked for his own profit, for people resent a person who works for his own advantage. But we must be careful not to build up our client too much; otherwise we will make our audience envious.

The above passage indicates a curious set of double standards. How wonderfully naïve it is to think that the good guys of the world all work to improve the advantage and the lot of others!

Cicero stresses the need to arouse the feelings and passions of the audience. Of course, it is only fair to say that Roman courts looked much more favorably upon character witnesses than we do. Regardless, the absence of the need for sound, careful, and logical thinking is startling.

The philosopher Dio Chrysostom (ca. A.D. 40–A.D. 112) writes lucidly about the tendency that people have to believe what they want to believe and to be complacent in their beliefs:

I know that it is difficult to teach people but that it is easy to deceive them. They learn with difficulty, and even when they do learn something from the few that know what they are talking about, they are deceived even more quickly by those who do not know what they are talking about. And they are deceived not only by others but even by themselves. For the truth is bitter and unpleasant to people who do not think, while things that are not true are sweet and attractive. One might draw an analogy to people who have sore eyes: when one's eyes are sore, it is painful to look at the light and it is comfortable to look into the darkness even though one can't see very much. . . . Now, as I have said, it is difficult for people to learn. But it is even more difficult for people to change their beliefs, especially when they have been hearing nonsense for a long time. . . . It is not easy to alter their opinions, regardless of how many arguments you have to prove their error.

It is easy to be wrong and at the same time completely convinced that we are right. Dio Chrysostom's image of the sore eyes is an apt one. How much more comfortable it is not to have to think but rather to accept and to be satisfied with appearances.

Michel de Montaigne (1533–1592) has a fine essay (Book I, Essay xxvii) on another human tendency: the tendency "to measure truth and error by our own capacity." [1]

It is perhaps not without reason that we consider credulity and the readiness to be persuaded to be signs of simplicity and ignorance. For I was once taught, I think, that belief is like an impression made upon the mind, and that the softer and less resistant the mind, the easier it is to impress something upon it. 'As the scale of the balance must necessarily sink when weights are placed upon it, so the mind must yield to clear proof.' The emptier a mind is, and the less counterpoise it has, the more easily it sinks under the weight of the first argument. That is why children, the common people, women, and the sick are particularly apt to be led by the ears. But then, on the other hand, it is a stupid presumption to go about despising and condemning as false anything that seems to us improbable; this is a common fault in those who think they have more intelligence than the crowd.

1. These excerpts from Montaigne are translated by J. M. Cohen in his collection of Montaigne's *Essays* published by Penguin Books.

Montaigne concludes the essay by showing how dangerous it is for people to form rash judgments and "to condemn what we do not understand." He tells an anecdote about certain things that he dismissed as nonsense. "But when I came to discuss them with learned men, I found that these things have a substantial and very solid foundation, and that it is only stupidity and ignorance that make us accept them with less reverence than the rest."

Francis Bacon, writing in the seventeenth century, identified four broad types of imprecise thinking. These are called his Four Idols:

> The Idols of the Tribe are errors in thinking that are common to most people.
>
> The Idols of the Cave are errors in thinking due to some personal bias, prejudice, and ignorance.
>
> The Idols of the Market Place are errors in thinking that come from a misunderstanding of words and language in the communication among people.
>
> The Idols of the Theater or Gallery are errors in thinking that come from a blind acceptance and unquestioned acceptance of attitudes and ideas.

René Descartes, also writing in the seventeenth century, recognizing the need for clear and precise thinking, enumerated four principles for careful thought. They are worth remembering:

> My first rule is to accept nothing as true that I do not clearly know to be true, to accept nothing more than is so clear and distinct that I cannot possibly doubt it.
>
> My second rule is to divide each issue or problem into as many parts as possible.
>
> My third rule is to begin with those elements of a problem or issue that are the simplest and easiest to understand and then to move gradually and by stages to the more complex.
>
> My fourth rule is to make my listings and enumerations so complete so as to have omitted nothing.

Descartes, then, stresses the following: the avoidance of bias and of blind acceptance and rash judgments; the need to analyze; the need to move gradually, logically, and methodically; and the need to be thorough.

I could continue to cite remarks from a wide range of other writers and thinkers, but I would be making the same points. Reason is indeed elusive. It is easy to be deceived. To avoid being deceived requires effort and vigilance, for the distinction between reason and the appearance of reason is often not obvious.

The Emotions

His tongue
Dropt Manna, and could make the worse appear
The better reason, to perplex and dash
Maturest Counsels: for his thoughts were low;
To vice industrious, but to Nobler deeds
Timorous and slothful; yet he pleas'd the ear.
Milton, *Paradise Lost*, II

Man is an emotional animal. This is often to the good. Without emotions our lives would be hopelessly drab and boring. The emotions complement our triumphs and defeats, and they add meaning to our lives. Constructively harnessed, they are the source of our greatest moments. Without them, we are brutes and automatons. They are essential in our interpersonal relationships, and they supply the motivation for everything we do in every aspect of our lives.

But in reasoned argument, the emotions often get in the way. They blind us from seeing clearly and from thinking objectively. Our emotions can trick us; because of them, we may accept as true that which is not true and we may be led astray to regard as relevant that which is not relevant. Our emotions can make us lose sight of what we are talking about.

We can view emotions from different vantage points: what to do so as not to pique the emotions of others and so as not to turn a neutral, if not benign, party into a hostile one; and what to recognize so that others will not take advantage of our emotions in order to deceive.

Sensitivity is the key word in dealing with others. We must at all costs remember that the other person has feelings. This may sound obvious, but it is frequently forgotten. Our emotions are delicate. We all have our weak spots; we are all vulnerable somewhere; rare is the person who does not feel some inadequacy. It is easy to hurt a person without wanting to do so and without even realizing that we have done so. Most people camouflage their feelings of inadequacy and their sensitive spots; hence, we may never know when we have stung one of those spots. If, for instance, I am conversing with a short person and I make a casual allusion, perhaps even a kindly one, to his shortness, I may momentarily hurt him. He may disregard my remark; he may even laugh it off. But, if he is sensitive to his height, my remark may create a slight barrier between us.

There is an adage: The truth hurts. People do not want to be reminded of their inadequacies or of their failures. It is one thing for them to recognize their weaknesses privately, but it is entirely different when someone else indicates that he is aware of those weaknesses.

Here is another type of situation. Harry has just had a fight with his wife and is venting his spleen to Joe. Harry calls his wife every name that he can think of and itemizes luridly each of her foibles. Joe, thinking that he is going along with Harry, then starts adding some of his own criticisms of Harry's wife. Suddenly there is a change in Harry's composure. "You've got no right to say those things about my wife!" flares forth Harry.

Harry's behavior seems totally irrational. Joe meant no harm. He was merely saying what he thought Harry wanted to hear. But he violated one of the basic codes of human intercourse: he invaded Harry's territory. There is a principle here: I can say whatever I want to say about myself, my family, or my friends. But you can't; and you had better not dare! You don't have that right.

If it is easy to offend people inadvertently, think of how easy it is to do so intentionally. One of the easiest ways to alienate someone is to make the other person lose face. When a person loses face, the issues suddenly become irrelevant. A new concern looms foremost; that person must regain and save face. If your intention is merely to make another person squirm, then go ahead and make him lose face; however, if your intention is to secure some agreement and understanding, then by all means be as sensitive as you can to the other person's feelings. Don't back him into a corner unless you are prepared to have him fight back.

Here are some of the specific ways that emotions can interfere with reasoned discussion:

We become personally involved; we regard as a personal attack an idea or attitude that differs from one of our own ideas or attitudes; we feel that, because something we say is challenged, we are personally being challenged.

We put the other person on the defensive by making dogmatic statements such as, "You don't know what you're talking about!" or "I know much more about this than you do."

We become sarcastic or patronizing or hostile.

We use language that is evaluative without defending or documenting those evaluations. We use loaded words, words that have strong emotional connotations.

Instead of addressing ourselves to the issue, we aim our remarks at the other person: at his weak spots, his personality, his style of presentation.

We make jokes at the expense of the other person.

We insult the other person.

We do not listen carefully to what the other person is saying; we select what suits our purpose and we reject what does not suit our purpose.

We consciously misinterpret what we hear; we take words or ideas out of context and twist those words and ideas.

We refuse to admit that the other person may have an occasional valid point and that there may be at least some truth in what he is saying.

When we are shown to be wrong, we rationalize or pass off the error as insignificant.

When we have proven someone else wrong, we crow and rub it in.

Any of the above dozen devices is sufficient to frustrate a negotiation and perhaps even to turn a discussion into a dispute.

So far we've dealt with discussions between people who are reasonable—people with a mutual desire to reach a conclusion, to come to an understanding, or to arrive at the truth. But people aren't always like that. Every now and then we meet someone who is simply unreasonable. With this person, all the delicacy, tact, sensitivity, and persuasiveness will do no good. There's an old saying: You can't argue with a drunk. If we regard *a drunk* as a synecdoche for a person who is closed-minded, who will not listen to reason, who is blinded by bias and prejudice, then don't argue. Unobstrusively change the subject or gracefully depart or merely fade into silence, letting the drunk have his own way. You can't win, and you'll only become angry.

We all have emotional needs: the need to love, to be loved, to be accepted, to feel a sense of accomplishment, to feel a sense of self-worth, to feel important, to feel needed, to protect ourselves, to attain status in our own eyes and in the eyes of others, to be secure. These needs, in turn, conceal other emotions: love, hate, fear, jealousy, anger, guilt, greed, hope, loyalty. The emotions are fragile and sensitive. They are easily tampered with and they are easily manipulated. A person who knows how to appeal to our emotions can deceive us, manipulate us, and get us to accept as true that which is untrue.

The following are some of the ways that the emotions are preyed upon in order to deceive reason. If we recognize them, we may be able to avoid deception and manipulation.

Appeal to pity (*argumentum ad misericordiam*). Instead of giving carefully documented reasons, evidence, and facts, a person appeals to our sense of pity, compassion, brotherly love. We are shown a picture of an emaciated child, a victim of malnutrition, and we are urged to send as large a donation as we can to a fund chartered to feed starving children. Now, there is nothing intrinsically wrong with such an appeal. But we should not be so naïve as to think that all of our donation will, in fact, go toward feeding a starving child. How much of that donation will be used for administration, for other advertisements, for plush salaries for the executives of the fund? The problem with this particular appeal to pity is that it does not tell us how our donation is going to be used and that it does not even assure us that the donation will be used for the purpose for which it was solicited.

The appeal to pity is often used in personal relationships. Mr. Brown's business is failing and he is trying to secure a bank loan. "If you don't give me the loan," he exclaims to the bank official, "I will have to declare bankruptcy. I'll be wiped out." This is sometimes an effective appeal, but it is not logically sound. The bank official would be a fool to authorize the loan unless he were convinced that Mr. Brown had enough business sense to use that loan productively.

A variation of the appeal to pity is the **plea for special treatment.** Sammy, a not particularly gifted basketball player, goes up to his coach: "You've got to let me play in tonight's game. My family is visiting me and they've never seen me play." Presuming that winning is most important, Sammy's plea is not a good reason to allow the boy to play, and, if the coach is a sensitive person, he is in an awkward position. Should he, against his better judgment, treat Sammy as a special case and risk losing the game?

The appeal to pity is a favorite rhetorical device. A fine example appears in a speech delivered by that famous lawyer Clarence Darrow. In 1924 he was defending Nathan Leopold and Richard Loeb, who were on trial for murder. The issue was not guilt; guilt had been established; rather, the issue was whether the two men should be executed or sentenced to life imprisonment.

> But there are others to consider. Here are these two families, who have led honest lives, who will bear the name that they bear, and future generations must carry it on.
>
> Here is Leopold's father—and this boy was the pride of his life. He watched him, he cared for him, he worked for him; the boy was brilliant and accomplished, he educated him, and he thought that fame and position awaited him, as it should have awaited. It is a hard thing for a father to see his life's hopes crumble into dust.
>
> Should he be considered? Should his brothers be considered? Will it do society any good or make your life safer, or any human being's life safer, if it should be handed down from generation to generation, that this boy, their kin, died upon the scaffold?

And Loeb's the same. Here are the faithful uncle and brother, who have watched here day by day, while Dickie's father and his mother are too ill to stand this terrific strain, and shall be waiting for a message which means more to them than it can mean to you or me. Shall these be taken into account in this general bereavement?

Have they any rights? Is there any reason, your Honor, why their proud names and all the future generations that bear them shall have this bar sinister written across them? How many boys and girls, how many unborn children will feel it? It is bad enough as it is, God knows. It is bad enough, however it is. But it's not yet death on the scaffold. It's not that. And I ask your Honor, in addition to all that I have said, to save two honorable families from a disgrace that never ends, and which could be of no avail to help any human being that lives.

Closely connected with the appeal to pity is the **appeal to guilt.** Let's return to a previous example. We are shown a picture of a starving child; then we are shown a picture of a comfortable family at the dinner table. "You don't have to worry," the advertisement proclaims; "you have all you need. You have it so good compared to the millions of starving people all over the world." We are invited to feel guilty because of our comfort. And, it is implied or perhaps even stated, we will feel even more guilty if we don't contribute. We are invited to think of that starving child the next time we bite into our supper. That image will haunt us until we donate.

Three points can be made about this appeal to guilt. First, no one has the right to prey upon our emotional balance. Second, unless sound reasons can be given for the speculation that we ought to feel guilty, that speculation is worthless. Third, even if we were to feel guilty, we have been given no reasons to do what the ad is suggesting; there is still no assurance that our donation will effect any palpable good.

The **appeal to fear** (*argumentum ad metum*) tries to frighten us into a specific action or into accepting a specific belief. "If you don't do X, then Y will happen." Of course, Y is something dreadful. "If you don't get the enemy first, he'll get you." But in order for the statement to have any validity, the speaker is obligated to show a specific cause and effect relationship between X and Y. For example, you bring your car to a garage for a tune-up; the mechanic says that the transmission is about to go, and he then proceeds to describe what will happen when the transmission does go. If the mechanic is unscrupulous, he is merely appealing to your sense of fear. In order for his claim to be sound, he is obliged to tell you specifically why he concludes that the transmission is faulty.

Sometimes the appeal to fear is personally directed. The protection racket employed by organized crime is an example. "See Billy's Bar? See what that freak fire did to it? Don't you think you should have protection in case the same thing should happen to you?" Sometimes the appeal is more subtle. For example, the overt or covert threat to an individual who does not conform to the wishes of a group: "Now, Doctor Hendricks, don't you realize that if you cause a stir about the fact that the steel mill is polluting the environment, the mill may have to close down. If it closes down, then thousands of people will be out of work. Surely you don't think that anyone will come to a doctor who is responsible for putting thousands of people out of work."

While I was preparing materials for this book, I received the following letter from a department store with which I have an account and which recently opened up an insurance department:

> Some people who receive this letter will not act on it. This amazes me. Perhaps because this protection offers such excellent value, I'm surprised that a Charge Customer like you would pass this up.
>
> Maybe I shouldn't be surprised. You may already have enough insurance to protect you against the dangers you face every day you travel. Maybe large medical expenses would be paid out of your savings. And, if your savings are large enough, even the thought of a long disability doesn't particularly worry you. If that's so, I'm glad you're so well protected.
>
> But why use your savings for expenses that could be paid by this insurance? Don't do it. Fill out and mail your application before this offer expires. That's all it takes. You send no money now.

The first paragraph contains an approach that will appear later in this chapter—the **appeal to sincerity.** Then there's a touch of flattery: If I'm a customer of X, then surely I have good sense; if I have good sense, surely I will see the wisdom of their insurance plan.

The second paragraph is the interesting one, a good example of the appeal to fear. That paragraph all but intimidates me. It clobbers me with innuendo and invites me to imagine horrible things. How much cheaper it would be in the long run to buy some peace of mind!

Appeal to hope. "If you do X, Y may happen; therefore, if you want Y to happen, do X." But there is no guarantee that Y will happen, nor are there any good reasons for claiming that X will have a significant effect upon Y. State lottery campaigns use this approach. We would all like to win $100,000, and when we are told of people who have won, especially when the "It can happen to you" pitch is used, our sense of hope may make us forget just how improbable are our chances of actually holding the winning ticket.

Appeal to flattery. When we are flattered, we tend to confuse our positive feelings toward the flatterer with what that person is actually saying. Beth flatters George; George is pleased with Beth's words; therefore, George is positively disposed toward Beth; therefore, George is more amenable to Beth's position. But note that Beth has offered no reasons for George to accept her position.

Appeal to status. Some people are very conscious of status. They flaunt their Gucci this, their Pucci that; they drive foreign cars; whenever they buy something, they regard the label of prime importance. These people feel that such outward manifestations of affluence will make them seem more important or more discriminating or more elegant or more worldly. These people are particularly susceptible to appeals that claim to enhance status: "An eloquent way to say you're special" proclaims an advertisement for a $150 ball point pen. Needless to say, a person gains distinction not by the products he uses but by his deeds. These people will look with disdain upon baked chicken with rice, but they will eagerly order the *arroz con pollo.*

Appeal to the bandwagon. This appeal is similar to the appeal to status. Instead of appealing to uniqueness, however, it appeals to our need to belong, to keep up with our neighbors. We are encouraged to travel abroad because that is what all the people of quality do. We were encouraged to buy a house in the country because our neighbors have a country house. On a more mundane level, "If ten million housewives are using Sparkle, shouldn't you too be using Sparkle!" Again, as with all emotional appeals, no good reasons have been given for going abroad, buying a country house, or using Sparkle. The only reason is to keep up with the others.

Then there is the **appeal to love** and its kid brother, the **appeal to trust.** Someone says that because you don't agree with him, you don't love him or you don't trust him. "Either you're with me or you're against me!" "If you really trusted me, then you'd go along with me." "If you were really my friend, then you'd agree with me." This approach is an unfair one. Whether you agree or disagree with a person has nothing to do with your fondness for that person. Not going along with a person does not necessarily mean that you do not love or that you do not trust that person. Before you accept any line of thought or consent to any course of action, you should first ascertain the reasons for accepting or consenting. Otherwise your actions may be irresponsible. The generic name for emotional appeals of this type is *argumentum ad amicitiam*—the **appeal to friendship.** We should remember that true friendship sometimes demands that we disagree.

Similar to the appeal to friendship is the **appeal to pride or loyalty** (*argumentum ad superbiam*). "If you are really proud of your country, if you really want to see her prosper and grow, then buy saving bonds." "What do you mean—you won't buy a ticket for the church raffle? What are you, against the church?" "You never take me out to dinner anymore; you're simply ashamed of me. You don't love me anymore." The appeal to pride or loyalty is usually a glaring oversimplification. Not buying savings bonds does not automatically mean that you're not loyal to your country. Not buying a raffle ticket does not automatically mean that you're not loyal to the church. Not taking your wife out to dinner does not automatically mean that you aren't proud of her or that you don't love her anymore.

Appeal to sincerity. This appeal can be very effective, especially when used by a good showman. A person adopts a very earnest, sincere, possibly self-effacing and certainly a humble tone. The person appears to be speaking from the absolute depths of his heart. He frequently pauses, as if he were struggling to find words to be able to express his next thought. His feelings are so deep that he can scarcely find words. He often repeats words for emphasis. The emphatic verb forms (forms with the auxiliaries *does* and *do*) and adverbs—*really, genuinely, truly, absolutely, actually*—are used to add to the feeling of sincerity:

> And so, ladies and gentlemen, I believe—I firmly believe— that this proposal is necessary. Very necessary. I do believe this. I have tried to be fair to the opposition, I really have. I have examined their position carefully. But I do feel that their proposal would wreak havoc with our economic system. Unnecessary havoc and irreparable havoc. I do think that, if they had taken the time to think out the implications of their idea, to think out what would happen two . . . three years from now if their ideas were implemented. . . .

Argumentum ad populum. This final emotional appeal embraces many—perhaps most—of the other appeals mentioned in this chapter. This is the *appeal to the crowd, to the mob, to the gallery.* Generalities, clichés, slogans, platitudes, sanctimonious claptrap, and glorification of the masses abound. Here is Harold Ickes, secretary of the interior, in 1941:

> What constitutes an American? Not color nor race nor religion. Not the pedigree of his family nor the place of his birth. Not the coincidence of his citizenship. Not his social status nor his bank account. Not his trade nor his profession. An American is one who loves justice and believes in the dignity of man. An American is one who will fight for his freedom and that of his neighbor. An American is one who will sacrifice prosperity, ease and security in order that he and his children may retain the rights of free men. An American is one in whose heart is engraved the immortal second sentence of the Declaration of Independence.
>
> Americans have always known how to fight for their rights and their way of life. Americans are not afraid to fight. They fight joyously in a just cause.
>
> We Americans know that freedom, like peace, is indi-

visible. We cannot retain our liberty if three-fourths of the world is enslaved. Brutality, injustice and slavery, if practiced as dictators would have them, universally and systematically, in the long run would destroy us as surely as a fire raging in our nearby neighbor's house would burn ours if we didn't help to put out his.

One of the most blatant examples of the *argumentum ad populum* is an advertisement for the Dodge Omni, an advertisement that may have gone too far in its appeal to the masses. Across a two-page spread appear the words M O M ' S   O M N I. On the left page is a picture of a clean-cut, attractive woman in her twenties or early thirties. She poses against a Dodge Omni with her two children, a boy and a girl. Then the spiel:

Seems like Omni was built for mom. To help her with her chores and errands. To pick up the gals for fun and games. And do it all without messing up her fuel budget.

EPA ESTIMATES:
39 MPG HIGHWAY/25 MPG CITY.

According to EPA estimates, Omni is rated 39 MPG (highway) and 25 MPG (city) when equipped with its standard 1.7 litre engine, four-speed manual transmission, and 3.3 transaxle ratio. That's very efficient going, even though mom's mileage may vary according to her car's condition and the way she drives. (A California mom's mileage is lower.)

And there's a lot more for moms to like about Omni. It's easy to handle and park, thanks to its front-wheel drive and precise rack-and-pinion steering. It has comfortable seating. There are optional soft touches like automatic transmission, air-conditioning, smart cloth upholstery, and lots more.

Dodge Omni has four wide-opening doors. And for any mom who's had to deal with a brace of grocery bags, or a bunch of kids, or just the general ins and outs of a day on the go ... those four doors become important.

Then there's Omni's hatchback. Open it up, and you're

confronted with a special storage compartment covered by a carpeted security panel. Into it you can put five, six, maybe seven bags of groceries. Four fully loaded golf bags. And all kinds of odds and ends . . . all tucked nicely out of sight. Or you can lift that hatchback, fold down the rear seat and security panel, and turn Omni into a station wagon with truly astounding cargo handling dimensions. For rocking chairs. Or fireplace wood. Or even playpens.

The patronizing tone that this ad conveys is enough to make one angry. The unctuous appeal to mom is offensive. The ad assumes that mom is a simpleminded lightweight who spends her day running chores, having fun and games with the gals, and acting the role of a mindless domestic. It's unlikely that the 3.3 transaxle ratio is going to mean very much to this plastic mom with a tooth-filled smile perpetually on her healthy face, but at least it sounds impressive. Who cares if mom doesn't know what it means! As long as she can get her five, six, or maybe seven bags of groceries into the back—or maybe even a playpen—what else matters!

Then there's the play on sound between *mOM* and *OMni*—at least that's got some subtlety to it. The rest is sheer appeal to the crowd, the crowd being, in this case, the housewife, but, alas, a very sorry stereotype of the housewife.

These are not the only devices that make up the broad area of emotionalism. There are also the areas of propaganda and suggestibility, topics that will be covered in later chapters. But these are the main appeals that are directed toward specific emotions.

Finally, it must be repeated, there is nothing inherently wrong with an emotional appeal. Sometimes such an appeal merely reflects a deep feeling or belief of a person who is unable to articulate the precise reasons behind that feeling or belief. The wife may be genuinely hurt by what she interprets as her husband's inattention to her, and her feeling may manifest itself in her emotional appeal to pride. The auto mechanic may honestly believe that your transmission is going to cause serious problems, and he may regard the appeal to fear as a short cut to get you to do what he feels is necessary. And the Dodge Omni may be a fabulous car. What is important is that you recognize that the emotional appeal may reflect some unstated feeling or belief, that there may be a bottom line that is not being articulated or a hidden agendum that is not being acknowledged. Perhaps the person trying to cajole you into buying a raffle ticket is genuinely interested in helping the church; on the other hand, perhaps he is merely trying to get rid of his quota of tickets. Always try to find the bottom line or to ascertain that hidden agendum. Feelings are important, but one should not act on feelings alone. One should have reasons for acting. It is in the obfuscation of reasons that emotional appeals are dangerous.

Propaganda

> *I know your race. It is made up of sheep. It is governed by
> minorities, seldom or never by majorities. It suppresses its
> feelings and its beliefs and follows the handful that
> makes the most noise. Sometimes the noisy handful is
> right, sometimes wrong; but no matter, the crowd follows
> it. The vast majority of the race, whether savage or civi-
> lized, are secretly kind-hearted and shrink from inflicting
> pain, but in the presence of the aggressive and pitiless
> minority they don't dare to assert themselves.*
>
> Mark Twain, *The Mysterious Stranger*, Chapter IX

We are tempted to regard propaganda as evil and propagandists as
sinister creatures. Nazi Germany springs to mind. We picture unscrupulous politicians, hysterical mobs, stentorian oratory, and precision parades.

Certainly, such images reflect a type of propaganda, but only a
type. In its broadest sense, propaganda is merely a type of persuasion, a type that appeals to our emotions rather than to our reason.
It relies upon suggestibility. It tries to get us to act or to think in a
certain way; it tries to influence our beliefs and eventually our
attitudes. Its means are often subtle and surreptitious. The propagandist does not lay his cards openly before us; as with most emotional appeals, there is a hidden agendum, a bottom line, that goes
unexpressed.

The propagandist realizes that we are more susceptible in a
crowd than in private. He knows that we are indeed influenced by
what others think and by what others are doing. He understands
that time is a valuable tool, that if people hear something often

enough, they are likely to be more receptive to it (hence the long-range advertising campaign). He realizes that if he can make us feel insecure and then provide us with something to remove that insecurity, we will listen to him more eagerly. He recognizes that if he can create a need, we will be more amenable to the means he suggests to satisfy that need.

Many advertisements and commercials exploit these techniques. We are threatened with the prospect of having body odor. "No one wants to have anything to do with a person who offends," the voice declaims disdainfully. But if we buy a particular brand of deodorant, the threat will be removed and we can conquer the world—or at least the brunette next door.

"If you *really* care, buy her X."

"Why isn't the Doyles' marriage as happy as the Greens'? Because Mrs. Doyle's hands look so shriveled. If she had been using the same dishwashing lotion that Mrs. Green has been using, her hands would look several years younger, and her marriage would be so much happier. After all, who can love a woman with dishpan hands?"

A full-page ad shows a bottle of whiskey. "At about $14, it's not everybody's bag." The ad suggests that only a special person—i.e., you—is discriminating enough to select that particular brand.

Another full-page ad shows a bottle of Wild Turkey bourbon. Tucked beneath the bottle is a note: "I love you." It is signed "Nancy." The caption: WILD VALENTINE FOR YOUR WILD GUY. Under that caption, the pitch: "In his wildest dreams, your man probably wouldn't expect a Valentine's Day greeting like this. Isn't that the best reason in the world to surprise him with the great Wild Turkey?" The unstated pitch: If you really want to see how wild he can be, loosen him up.

A particularly interesting ad comes from an organization seeking financial aid for education: "Have you any idea how much America's colleges mean to you?" Then the following commentary:

It was college-based research and college-trained minds that gave us electronic computers, television, spacecraft. That conquered polio, smallpox, diphtheria. That developed new strains of rice and wheat to help feed the world's hungry.

And it will be today's college-trained minds that will solve tomorrow's problems: Energy. Transportation. Health. City planning. International relations.

But only if you help. America's colleges are in deep financial trouble. They cannot train minds for tomorrow unless you make it possible now. So give them a hand. The help you give today will make tomorrow's world a better one.

Since when is health a problem? And isn't it assuring to know that your contribution *will* make the world a better one. The oversimplification here is comic.

Some people insist that no one pays any attention to these ads, but that's not true. If we hear of the dangers of body odor often enough, we may well be tempted to seek protection. If the housewife sees that her hands are not as glamorous as they used to be, she may try a particular dishwashing liquid, hoping to restore her hands to their former luster. And if enough people associate status with a certain whiskey label, we may be tempted to put that label conspicuously on our shelves.

A successful propagandist preys upon our emotions. He uses many of the emotional appeals cited in the previous chapter. He tells us what we want to hear, wins our confidence, and then subtly begins to influence our attitudes. The propagandist rarely gives good reasons for what he is advocating. If he does give evidence, it is selective, one-sided. He oversimplifies and often misrepresents.

The following discussion details some of the devices used by the propagandist:

The bandwagon. "Everyone is doing it. Therefore, you should be doing it too." Of course, the statement is an oversimplification. Everyone is not doing it. The bandwagon works on at least two levels. First of all, it tries to give the impression that a lot of people are doing something or supporting some position; then it suggests that the judgment of the masses is sound: If so many people are doing it, then it must be right. Second, and more important, the bandwagon is an emotional appeal to our need for belonging. We don't want to be left out. "So, hop on the bandwagon. Join the crowd and be happy and secure."

Repetition. The propagandist says something over and over again. He may use different words each time, but it's the same point. The theory is that if you say something often enough, people will eventually believe you.

Confidence. The propagandist also speaks confidently. He gives the impression of knowing what he is talking about. His voice is strong; his facial expressions are bold; his bodily gestures are decisive. The theory here is something like this: If this person is so confident, if he is so sure of his position, he must be right. People prefer to support a winner, and a confident manner makes a person look like a winner.

Earnestness and **sincerity** are two additional features. The more earnest and sincere a person appears, the more readily will he be believed.

Oversimplification. The propagandist takes one side of a situation and treats that one side as if it were the only side. A political candidate, for instance, may mention only the weak points of his opponent, completely ignoring his opponent's strong points. He takes a complex issue and reduces it to extremes, often presenting that issue as an *either . . . or:* "Either you go along with me, and that will be to the good of everyone, or you don't, and that, of course, will be disastrous." I have *the* solution, he implies, ignoring the fact that rarely is there ever *one* solution to a complex problem. Similarly, if he is talking about an existing problem, he will oversimplify the causes of that problem: "It is all because of . . ." Of course, the act of oversimplifying is an act of distortion.

Name-calling. The propagandist assigns abusive epithets or uses names that have strong pejorative emotional associations to people or ideas he doesn't like, and he assigns flattering epithets or uses names that have strong positive emotional associations to people or ideas he does like. He expects his names to influence our attitudes. Sometimes he will use **labels**: "racist," "anarchist," "socialist," "radical," "reactionary." These labels may indeed be effective in biasing his audience, but they should be suspect unless he has first defined the term and then offered evidence.

Stereotyping. This is a variation of name-calling and of oversimplification. The propagandist takes one characteristic of a person, exaggerates it, and then regards it as the only characteristic. This technique was sometimes used against the late senator and former vice-president, Hubert Humphrey, who was occasionally caricatured as a windbag. True, Humphrey did like to talk. But he often did have things of significance to say. The stereotype strips a person of his complexity and his individuality and reduces him to one quality.

The glittering generality. The propagandist makes broad, sweeping statements, usually ones with complex and far-reaching ramifications, but he ignores the complexities and the ramifications. "We must have tax reform," he pontificates. "The poor of this country have borne the brunt of the tax burden long enough." And then he blasts the opposition for exploiting the poor and for not securing effective tax-reform legislation. But he himself offers no specifics. He basks in the complacencies of his generalities. The glittering generality is safe: How can someone be criticized when he offers no specifics?

Slogans. The audience will remember the clever slogan without challenging the meaning of the slogan—in fact, without even thinking about the meaning or the ramifications of the slogan: America—Love It or Leave It. Make Love, Not War. When Guns Are Outlawed, Only Outlaws Will Have Guns.

Transfer. This technique encourages us to transfer our emotions from one source to another. Cigarette advertisements constantly use this technique. In the background of an ad is the Grand Canyon; in the foreground is a pack of L&Ms. THE PROUD SMOKE, claims the headline, PRODUCT OF A PROUD LAND. Then the caption: "Tobacco. It's as proud a part of the American tradition as the Grand Canyon. At Liggett & Myers, we've made tobacco into a cigarette worthy of that tradition. The rich, mellow, distinctively smooth L&M. Smoke it proudly." Look through almost any magazine and find the KOOL advertisement; the cigarette is invariably set in some lush country scene, couched in deep greens. Then there is the Marlboro Man and the Virginia Slims lady: "You've come a long way, baby." The transfer technique realizes that we are proud of our land, that we yearn for the beauty of the country, and that we admire the rugged Marlboro Man and the svelte Virginia Slims' lady, and it invites us to transfer our positive feelings to the object that is being promoted.

Testimonial. This is a variation of the transfer technique. An important or prominent person or organization speaks in behalf of an idea or a product. We are encouraged to support that idea or product merely because the prominent person speaks for it. The theory is something like this: X is an important person; X wouldn't be important unless he were better or more knowledgeable than we; since he is important, he is therefore better or more knowledgeable than we; therefore, he knows what he is talking about; therefore, we should believe him. We are encouraged to transfer our approval of that person toward the idea or product that he is endorsing.

Plain folks. "I'm just like one of you." The propagandist sometimes tries to win our support by getting us to identify with him. He comes to town meetings, visits hospitals, and poses informally for photographs. President Jimmy Carter used this technique when he appeared on television dressed in a casual sweater instead of a formal suit. Here the technique was used for honorable ends: energy conservation. If the President conserves energy by dressing sensibly, shouldn't we all?

The example just cited demands an important comment. Propaganda can be used for noble as well as for ignoble ends. Again, let me repeat the definition: Propaganda is merely a type of persuasion.

The theory behind the plain-folks technique holds that if we can identify with a person, we can support what he is saying. The technique is a variation of transfer.

Commercials, of course, exploit this technique. The "Man-on-the-street" is a typical approach. Then there is a brand of apple pie "just like Grandma used to make," and the frequent presentation of the typical housewife whose use of a certain product has made her so much happier or freer.

Snob appeal. On the other hand, propaganda may exploit a person's need for status or his desire to feel special: "For the person of discriminating taste" . . . "Not for everyone" . . . "Quality for the person of quality" . . . "A touch of elegance" . . . "For the person who cares enough to give the very best."

Statistics without context. The propagandist may give you plenty of statistics, but he rarely gives you the background of those statistics. He rarely tells you how he gathered them, where they came from, or how many people were polled. You can get 80 percent of the people to support virtually anything if you ask the right five people.

Large numbers. This is a variation of the bandwagon technique.

An advertisement for L'Oréal Hair Colouring (note the pretentious spelling!) claims, "More than 250,000 hairdressers the world over believe in what L'Oréal Hair Colouring can do for you. What more can we say? L'OREAL: A quarter-million hairdressers can't be wrong." A wonderful example of the large numbers technique appears in a Volkswagen ad. The headline: WHY THE VW RABBIT IS THE #1 SELLING IMPORTED CAR IN DETROIT. The blurb: "If people in Detroit know about anything, they know about cars. Cars are what they eat, breathe, and think. And when they think about imported cars, they buy VW Rabbits most." Apparently neither 250,000 hairdressers nor the people of Detroit can be wrong!

The manufactured problem—the bad guy, the scapegoat. The propagandist creates or exaggerates a problem, tries to convince you how serious the problem is, and then appeases you by blaming someone for that problem or by suggesting that his proposal will solve the problem. The propagandist often needs a bad guy, a victim or a scapegoat, someone whom he can lambaste. His indignation makes him sound sincere, and it makes the problem that he is talking about sound serious and urgent.

Arrant distortion. Sometimes the propagandist selects his information to present a one-sided view; sometimes he may even make up data to suit his own purposes; sometimes he simply lies. Since we do not have the true facts, there is no way we can challenge him. Since we are helpless, the cards are stacked against us and for him; hence, this technique is sometimes known as **card-stacking**.

The command. This technique is a dangerous one, for it can easily backfire. Some people are comfortable when they are being told what to do. When the propagandist gives a command, he is appealing to this need for authority.

Again, it must be emphasized, there is nothing intrinsically wrong with propaganda just as there is nothing intrinsically wrong with emotional appeals. But it is important that we know propaganda for what it is and not allow ourselves to be manipulated by it.

6

Suggestion

The clever reader who is capable of reading be-
tween these lines what does not stand written in
them but is nevertheless implied will be able to form
some conception.

Goethe, *Autobiography*

When you suggest something, you say something that operates on at least two different levels. Your words make a specific statement, but behind that statement is another more implicit statement. Your statement implies more than it says. It hints; it reflects a belief or an attitude that is not specifically articulated. A suggestion may put an idea into the mind of the listener; it invites him to make an inference; and it invites him to accept a belief or attitude without actually verbalizing that invitation.

There are a variety of ways to effect suggestion. **The hint** can be painfully obvious or artfully subtle. When a person hints, he may be testing the ground, trying to ascertain how receptive another person will be to what he wants, putting forth bait and seeing whether the other person will react to the bait. Or he may use the hint to try to seed the other person's mind.

Allen and Anne are dating. "Let's go to my place where we can be more comfortable," Allen says, hoping to get Anne to a setting where they can "make out" but hesitant to actually say what is on his mind. If Anne eagerly agrees, Allen feels much more confident and hopeful. If she is apprehensive, Allen realizes that he will have to be careful. And if she says no, at least Allen hasn't lost face: Anne has not refused his advances; she has merely said that she would rather not go to his place. The hint has allowed Allen to test the ground without actually having to commit himself.

A husband and wife pass a jewelry store. "What a beautiful necklace!" the wife exclaims. She may want the necklace but be reluctant to ask her husband for it. Her comment allows the husband to take the initiative. If he doesn't react, at least she hasn't been hurt with a refusal.

Some people can speak their minds directly and can accept a candid answer without feeling uncomfortable. Many others, however, find it difficult to express themselves directly in language; they need a protective barrier. The hint supplies that protection. People will rely upon a hint because they may lack confidence, because they may have a fear of rejection or a fear of being hurt, because a flat no might indicate a finality that they do not want, or because they find language inadequate to their own feelings.

Sometimes the hint may backfire, for, like any element of suggestion, it is subject to misinterpretation. Nonetheless, for some people, it is a useful shield, a means to avoid commitment. Words can be cold and clinical and can come out wrong, and it is much easier, perhaps much safer, for some people to be indirect rather than direct.

There's more to be said about this. We often have a conflict between our conscience and our instincts. In the Anne/Allen example mentioned above, it is possible that Anne's conscience tells her that she should not make out with Allen but that her instincts tell her that she would like to. If Allen uses the words, "Do you want to make out?" she will be able to make a conscious choice, her conscience may prevail, and she may refuse his request. But if no words are used, if Allen's approach is a gradual one, Anne may be able to suspend the dictates of her conscience and allow her instincts, i.e., her true desires, to supersede her conscience. Therefore, the hint may be as useful for Anne as it is for Allen. To what extent there will be qualms or even regrets the next morning is another question.

Accent. One can suggest a great deal merely by accenting a particular word. Note, for instance, the following statement: "I never try to cheat on my income tax." If the speaker stresses the *I*, he may be implying that you, or others, do try to cheat. If he emphasizes *try*, he may be implying that he does sometimes inadvertently cheat. If he emphasizes *cheat*, he may imply that he does not actually cheat but that he does cut corners. If he emphasizes *my,* he may suggest that he does try to cheat when he prepares someone else's tax return. If he stresses *income,* he may imply that he does cheat in other areas of taxation. And if he accents *income tax,* he may suggest that, while he doesn't cheat on his income tax return, he does cheat in other areas.

Of course, if the statement appears in print, then a reader can twist the original by accenting.

Selection. A person may try to effect a certain belief by selecting his evidence. A mother asks her son, "How are you doing in English this term?" He responds buoyantly, "Oh, I just got a ninety-five on a quiz." The statement conceals the fact that he has failed every other quiz and that his actual average is 55. Yet, if she pursues the matter no further, the mother may be delighted that her son is doing so well.

Linda asks Susan, "Have you read much Dickens?" Susan responds, "Oh, *Pickwick Papers* is one of my favorite novels." The statement may disguise the fact that *Pickwick Papers* is the only novel by Dickens that she has read, and it may give Linda the impression that Susan is a great Dickens' enthusiast.

Tone of voice. Our tone of voice may suggest a belief or an attitude without our having to come right out and explicitly state that belief or attitude. A teacher catches a student smoking in the bathroom. He realizes that he has to report that student, but, at the same time, he likes the student and doesn't want the full weight of the law to fall upon that student. Therefore, he gently enters the principal's office: "I'm afraid that I have something unfortunate to tell you," he remarks in a soft and plaintive tone. "I just came across Teddy Jones smoking—and he's been doing so well lately." The teacher has used three techniques here: (1) his low-keyed approach and his gentle tone of voice suggest that the matter is not a very serious one; (2) his euphemism "came across" instead of "caught" tries to remove some of the sting from the situation; (3) "and he's been doing so well lately" tries to bias the principal in favor of the student. The teacher has not specifically said that he wants the principal to be lenient, but his presentation has certainly invited the principal to be lenient.

On the other hand, the teacher may aggressively enter the principal's office and in a severe, sharp tone of voice state, "I've just caught Jones smoking in the bathroom." The teacher has not explicitly said that he wants the boy to be treated harshly, but he has certainly put the principal in that frame of mind.

Phraseology. The way one phrases a statement can be suggestive. The two different approaches which could be used by the teacher in the above example illustrate this principle. The second approach, by using the strong verb *caught* and by referring to the boy as Jones instead of Teddy Jones, suggests a strongly disapproving attitude.

The statements "Betty is late" and "Betty hasn't arrived yet" may have the same denotative meaning, but the first statement suggests a disapproving attitude and the second suggests a neutral attitude.

Bertrand Russell devised a system to illustrate how statements can suggest attitudes. He playfully called this system "conjugating an irregular verb." An example:

> I am firm.
> You are obstinate.
> He is a pig-headed fool.

Each of these three statements suggests something different:

> I am firm, and that is a good thing.
> You are obstinate, and that's not a very good thing.
> He is a pig-headed fool, and that's a very bad thing.

A classic illustration of the way equivalent statements may be phrased to suggest different attitudes is the following pair:

> The pitcher is half full.
> The pitcher is half empty.

The statements make the same assertion, but each expresses a different attitude. Note the following statement: Daisy is fatter than Debby. Most people hearing this would assume that Daisy is fat. Such an assumption is not necessarily true. The only thing that the sentence says is that Daisy is fatter than Debby; it does not say that either Daisy or Debby is fat. In the same way, the statement could have been phrased: Debby is thinner than Daisy. Now we picture two relatively thin girls. But, again, the statement does not say that either Debby or Daisy is thin; it merely says that one is thinner than the other.

Word choice can be important. Several words may have the same denotative meaning, but each word may conjure a different image: *svelte, slender, thin, lean, skinny; odor, smell, aroma, scent; innocent, naïve, ingenuous, credulous, gullible. Bureaucrat,* instead of *office worker; functionary,* instead of *official; sawbones,* instead of *surgeon.* Such loaded words actually evaluate while pretending merely to define.

We must be careful to distinguish between words that objectively describe and words that subjectively evaluate. Mr. Thayer says to Mr. Simmons, "Oh, by the way, we have a new person in the office, Rik Rollins. I gather you know him." Mr. Simmons replies, "Sure I do. He's a real jerk." Now, Simmons has biased Thayer against Rollins. The word *jerk* means nothing; it merely expresses a disapproving attitude. Too often that unfavorable attitude goes unchallenged. Thayer and Simmons move on to a new subject of discussion, and Simmons is less positively disposed toward Rollins.

Adjectives and adverbs require special alertness. We must always determine whether they are being used to describe or to qualify or whether they are actually evaluating something or someone. When I say "The apple is green," I am using the adjective *green* to describe. However, when I say "Herb was absolutely green with envy," I am using the adjective *green* to evaluate and to pass judgment on Herb's behavior. Unless Herb specifically states that he is highly envious, I do not know that he is envious. At best, I can make an inference, and there is no guarantee that that inference will be valid. When I say that he was green with envy, I am passing off inference as fact, and you, the listener, may accept it as fact. When I say that Ben entered the room cautiously, I am making an inference. It may appear to me that Ben is walking cautiously, but I do not know that he is in fact being cautious. The adverb *cautiously* is another example of an inference parading as a fact.

When you hear an adjective or an adverb, do not automatically accept as fact the judgment that that word implies. Don't accept evaluations implied by adjectives or adverbs unless they are accompanied by good reasons.

Another device of suggestion is **metaphor.** If I use the phrase

"And then Vivian slinked up to Biff," the metaphor in *slinked* suggests much more than the words actually express. Not only am I implicitly accusing Vivian of trying to be seductive but I am also inducing you to accept that accusation. Not only am I expressing a disapproving attitude toward Vivian but I am also trying to get you to adopt that attitude. A metaphor is often used to create an emotional bias without defending or giving reasons to support that bias. Again, judgment parades as fact. Metaphor indeed adds life and color to the language, but it can also be used unfairly, suggesting more than the speaker has a right to suggest.

Juxtaposition. Two statements are made. No connection is expressed. But because of the proximity of the two statements, a connection is suggested. Headline: MAYOR DECIDES NOT TO RUN FOR A THIRD TERM. Subhead: City Close To Bankruptcy. Nowhere is it stated that the mayor is responsible for the city's financial condition, but the reader is certainly tempted to make that inference.

Sometimes an **irrelevant detail** is inserted to bias the audience. A news commentator reports as follows: "The Metropolitan Charities Association of our city is about to begin its annual citywide campaign for contributions. The association recently moved its offices to 335 Park Avenue, one of the poshest areas of town." Through that last phrase, "one of the poshest areas of town," the commentator is suggesting a great deal: Why are the charity's offices in such an exclusive part of the city? If the association can afford offices in such an expensive neighborhood, how is it spending its money? But note, though the news commentator has not candidly expressed his concern, through insinuation he has invited his audience to form a conclusion. Now, it is very possible that the hypothetical Metropolitan Charities Association is feathering its own bed. If that is true, it is the responsibility of the newsman to get his facts and to present those facts. Otherwise, he is acting irresponsibly.

A leading national magazine did an article on the controversial drug Laetrile. The following are a few excerpts:

> Laetrile's origins go back to the 1920s, when Dr. Ernst Krebs, a San Francisco physician, was looking for a substance to improve the flavor of bootleg whiskey. On a hunch, he turned his attention to finding a substance that

would cure cancer and eventually discovered a crude apricot extract that seemed to have an antitumor effect in rats. However, it quickly proved of doubtful value for use in humans. Then in 1949, Ernst Krebs, Jr., a biochemist and medical-school dropout, purified his father's extract and isolated the active ingredient.

Next to Krebs, the major figure in the Laetrile movement is the 60-year-old Andrew McNaughton. . . . A picaresque entrepreneur who acted as a double agent in the Castro Cuban revolt and once sold arms to [a foreign country], he started a foundation for the exploration of offbeat scientific theories. After a 1956 meeting with Krebs in a Miami drugstore, McNaughton made Laetrile the No. 1 item on the foundation's agenda.

Now, reread the passage, noting the following phrases:

—Looking for a substance to improve the flavor of bootleg whiskey
—On a hunch
—Medical-school dropout
—A picaresque entrepreneur who acted as a double agent in the Castro Cuban revolt and once sold arms to [a foreign country]
—Offbeat scientific theories
—In a Miami drugstore

Each of these phrases may be true, but in this context they are irrelevant. They do, however, help to create a bias against Laetrile. Our feelings are manipulated by these irrelevant and loaded phrases.

Then there are IMAGE WORDS. A positive image word is one that tries to make things sound better than they actually are or that t ies to remove the sting from a possibly unpleasant condition. A glaring example is the phrase "senior citizens" for old people. Names similar to Floral Gardens, Sylvan Mansions, or Woodland Estates are often selected for nondescript housing developments. (Many bearing such names are, of course, lovely places to live.) A ball point pen is called a *writing instrument.* A spokesman for the military comments as follows:

> Last night the 43rd Battalion engaged in a series of protective reaction strikes, terminating several bands of denizens and supplementing said incursion with predirected air support. Friendly fire was minimized and strategically undirected targeting occurred only in low priority areas.

How does this translate?

> Last night the 43rd Battalion attacked several villages and killed a lot of people. It was assisted by bombings from aircraft. Some innocent people were killed, but not too many. And while some of the bombs missed their marks, not too much damage was done.

The euphemisms of the military spokesman try to camouflage the fact that botches occurred and innocent people were killed.

Pompous language—sometimes called *jargonese* or *doublespeak*—is often used to make the mundane and the trivial seem important. A study of a wilderness area in Montana reports: "A multidimensional concept of a wildernism-urbanism continuum replaced a comfort-continuing concept in defining the functional relationships among the components of the model."

When the writer of that sentence was questioned about its meaning and about its unnecessary verbiage, he replied that he was trying to express a very complex concept that is "not yet ready for publication in the *Reader's Digest."* Virtually no one can accept such a prose construction; it's just inflated language and warrants being dismissed as *gobbledygook.*

Negative image words, on the other hand, have the opposite effect. They make things sound worse than they may actually be. "The Red Sox were massacred last night." "Such a pea-brain has no right to run for office." "This place is a dump."

Suggestion is sometimes induced by **phrasing a question in a controlling fashion.** The phrases *you do, don't you, surely you,* and their equivalents try to control the response before that response can be made. If the question is posed firmly and dogmatically, it is even more loaded. "You don't really want to go out tonight, do you?" makes it more difficult for you to say, "Yes, I do want to go out."

Another example: The scene is a political gathering, and the people are trying to ascertain the candidate's views on various subjects. Mr. Turner asks a question: "Sir, I'd like to know how you feel about the school issue. As you know, there is a strong move to relocate the high school. But many of us feel just as strongly that the high school should stay just where it is. If it were moved, most of the people in this room would be unnecessarily inconvenienced ... to say nothing about the added burden on our city taxes. Now, what is your position?"

If Mr. Turner's intention is to try to get the candidate to respond in a particular way, then his question may be aptly phrased. But if his intention is to learn the candidate's true feelings about the issue, then he has phrased his question foolishly. The candidate immediately knows what answer the audience is looking for, and he can reply with sufficient discretion so as not to offend.

When we use emotional or suggestive language, we express our approval or disapproval through our words and through our tone of voice. We often do so, however, without giving solid reasons for our attitudes. Then, the people who hear our words may themselves be tempted to accept our attitudes or our beliefs without examining the reasons behind them. The reasons may be unsound, weak, biased, prejudiced, or unfair; there may be no good reasons, but the emotional and suggestive language has disguised that fact. People may unquestioningly accept what we say because of the intensity of our language. Emotional language invariably tells more about the speaker than about what the speaker is saying.

Reasoning

Always to be right, always to trample forward, and
never to doubt, are these not the great qualities with
which dullness takes the lead in the world?
            Thackeray, *Vanity Fair,* XXXV

A fallacy is an error in thinking or reasoning. Strictly speaking, it is
not an error in fact or belief. It involves *thought process;* therefore,
it pertains to conclusions, not to the statements that form those
conclusions. Furthermore, the word *fallacy* usually applies to conclusions that appear sound and that are often convincing but are, in
fact, incorrect.

Another word for thought process is *argument.* An argument is
a series of statements; some of these statements are *premises:* assertions, reasons, claims; from these premises is derived a *conclusion.*
The argument claims that, because the premises are true, the conclusion is true. If the conclusion does indeed logically follow from
the premises, the argument is *valid;* if the conclusion does not logically follow from the premises, the argument is *invalid.* Note that
the words "valid" and "invalid" apply to conclusions or to arguments, not to premises. When we refer to premises, we describe
them as being true or untrue.

Whenever we want to evaluate an argument, we should examine both the premises and the conclusions. The premises, i.e., the
evidence, should be thorough and accurate; the conclusion should
clearly and incontrovertibly derive from that evidence. When an
argument is unsuccessful, it has probably gone wrong in one of the
following areas:

1. The evidence has not been thorough; contradictory evidence has been overlooked or ignored.

2. The evidence has not been accurate; false or unsubstantiated or misleading statements have been claimed as fact.

3. The conclusion has not clearly and incontrovertibly come from the evidence; the relationship between evidence and conclusion has not been a firm one.

When one or more of these phenomena occur in an argument, that argument is said to be fallacious. The argument claims to have done something that it in fact has not done.

Another way to describe arguments is to determine whether they are *sound* or *unsound*. To be sound (1) the premises must be true and (2) the conclusions must logically follow from these premises. If either of these conditions is violated, the argument is unsound.

Let us look at five types of arguments:

1. The premises are true and the conclusion logically derives from those premises.

> All gorillas are mammals.
> Bobo is a gorilla.
> Therefore, Bobo is a mammal.

The argument is both sound and valid.

2. At least one of the premises is false, but the conclusion logically follows from the premises.

> All gorillas are man-eaters.
> Bobo is a gorilla.
> Therefore, Bobo is a man-eater.

This argument is unsound but valid. Since the first statement is not true, the argument is not sound. But, since the conclusion logically does follow from those premises, the argument is valid. If all goril-

las were man-eaters, then, indeed, Bobo the gorilla would be a
man-eater.

3. The premises are true, but the conclusion does not logically
follow from those premises.

> All gorillas are mammals.
> Bobo is a mammal.
> Therefore, Bobo is a gorilla.

This argument is unsound and invalid. Bobo could be a whale or a
monkey or a human and still be a mammal.

4. At least one of the premises is false, and the conclusion does
not follow.

> All mammals are dangerous.
> Bobo is dangerous.
> Therefore, Bobo is a mammal.

This argument is also unsound and invalid. It is unsound because
the first premise is not true. It is invalid because the conclusion
does not logically derive from the premises: Bobo could be a snake.

5. At least one of the premises is false, but the conclusion is
true.

> All humans are animals.
> Most animals can climb trees.
> Therefore, most humans can climb trees.

In spite of the fact that the conclusion is true, the argument is both
unsound and invalid. The fact that the conclusion is true is merely a
coincidence: it does not logically follow from the premises. Merely
substitute "dogs" for "humans" and you will see why the argument
is invalid.

Note that the word *fallacy* is sometimes broadly used to describe an error in belief. Thus the statement, "People on welfare
don't really want to work," might loosely be called fallacious.

Technically, however, it is merely untrue. Such a statement can be considered a fallacy, however, because it is usually the conclusion of some unstated premises. For instance:

a. If the people on welfare really wanted to work, they would find jobs.
    But they don't find jobs.
    Therefore, they don't really want to work.

or

b. All the people I know who are on welfare don't really want to work.
    Therefore, all people on welfare don't want to work.

Actually, the second example has an additional unstated premise:

c. All the people I know who are on welfare accurately represent the position of all people on welfare.
    All the people I know who are on welfare don't really want to work.
    Therefore, all people on welfare don't really want to work.

It is very important, therefore, to realize that both correct and incorrect beliefs are based on some premises, and it is crucial to determine just what those premises are. Only when the premises are first exposed and then examined can the worth of the conclusion be determined.

When anything goes wrong in the reasoning process, we have a fallacy. Fallacies can be *formal;* i.e., there may be something wrong with the form of the argument, with the way the argument is set up. Let us look back at argument *c* above:

All the people I know who are on welfare accurately represent the position of all people on welfare.
All the people I know who are on welfare don't really want to work.
Therefore, all people on welfare don't really want to work.

Is this argument valid? In other words, if the premises were true, would the conclusion be a valid one?

This question may present difficulties to most people. The argument sounds good; but is it? Does that conclusion incontrovertibly come from those premises. Examining the form of the argument will clarify the issue. There are three terms to the argument:

> People I know who are on welfare. (Call this term X.)
> All people who are on welfare. (Call this term Y.)
> People who don't want to work. (Call this term Z.)

Here is the form of the argument:

d. All X is Y.
   All X is Z.
   Therefore, all Y is Z.

Now, to test the form of this argument, we will substitute a different set of objects for X, Y, and Z—a set of objects that will be clear-cut—and we will make sure that we form true statements. Let us say that X refers to *cats,* that Y refers to *mammals,* and that Z refers to *instinctively chasing mice.* Using the form of the argument cited above, we have

e. All cats are mammals.   (All X is Y.)
   All cats instinctively chase mice.   (All X is Z.)
   Therefore, all mammals instinctively chase mice.   (All Y is Z.)

Can you imagine horses and cows and pigs chasing mice? Just as the conclusion to argument *e* is invalid, so the conclusion to argument *c* has to be invalid. Any argument that has the form described in *d* is going to be invalid. We will say more about such formal fallacies in Chapters 20 and 21.

Informal fallacies, on the other hand, are errors in reasoning. Informal fallacies occur because of rash or incorrect or careless inferences or because an argument contains a premise that is untrue or weak and the untruth or weakness of that premise goes unnoticed. There are many ways to classify informal fallacies, but the most appealing categories are those of irrelevance, confusion, and oversimplication. In the first category, a conclusion is based on some statement that is irrelevant. In the second category, an incorrect conclusion is reached because of ambiguity or because of confusion in the meanings of words or in the handling of an idea. In the third category, people jump to hasty conclusions and do not examine an issue carefully enough.

The following chapters discuss various types of fallacies. The list may seem overwhelming at times. It is not meant to be so; rather, we are merely attempting to isolate and to itemize different types of muddled thinking. The organization is often arbitrary: An item under one heading might just as well have been included under a different heading. Furthermore, when there is duplication, that duplication is intentional.

Finally, you might be tempted to ask, "Why are there so many fallacies?" "Why is there so much muddled thinking?" The answers appear at the end of Chapter 2. Reread those principles, and keep them in mind as you read the following chapters.

Irrelevance

> *"Harkee, landlord," said the sergeant, "don't abuse the cloth,*
> *for I won't take it." "D——n the cloth,". answered the landlord;*
> *"I have suffered enough by them." "Bear witness, gentlemen,"*
> *says the sergeant; "he curses the king, and that's high treason."*
> *"I curse the king! You villain," said the landlord. "Yes you*
> *did," cries the sergeant, "you cursed the cloth, and that's curs-*
> *ing the king. It's all one and the same, for every man who*
> *curses the cloth would curse the king if he durst; so for matter o'*
> *that, it's all one and the same thing." "Excuse me there, Mr.*
> *Sergeant," quoth Partridge, "that's a* non sequitur." *"None of*
> *your outlandish linguo," answered the sergeant, leaping from*
> *his seat; "I will not sit still and hear the cloth abused." "You*
> *mistake me, friend," cries Partridge, "I did not mean to abuse*
> *the cloth; I only said your conclusion was a* non sequitur."
> *"You are another," cries the sergeant, "an you come to that. No*
> *more a* sequitur *than yourself. You are a pack of rascals, and*
> *I'll prove it, for I will fight the best man of you all for twenty*
> *pound."*
>
> Fielding, *Tom Jones*, IX, 6

There is a surprising amount of irrelevance in both public and private discussion. Far too many of us are easily sidetracked from the issue at hand. Many of the emotional appeals cited earlier—the appeals to fear and to pity, or to flattery, friendship, pride, guilt, trust, and hope—are irrelevant. These appeals are often persuasive, but they do not constitute good reasons for accepting a position. For instance, when a father says to his son, "If you don't mow the lawn, you can't have the car tonight," he is not giving his son a good reason for mowing the lawn. He is merely describing what will happen if the son doesn't mow the lawn. Of course, if the son wants to use the car, he will get the lawn mowed; nonetheless, he will not be doing it for a sound reason.

Here are additional types of irrelevance, many of them variations of the emotional and suggestive appeals already mentioned.

One of the most common types of irrelevant appeals is the **argumentum ad hominem,** the argument directed against the speaker rather than toward what the speaker is saying. An example of this type of appeal is the **abusive ad hominem** argument: The personality of someone is criticized or attacked instead of what the person is saying. The theory is something like this: X is proposing Y; but X is a scoundrel, or X has done something that merits our disapproval; therefore, if we disapprove of X or of what X has done, then we have to disapprove of what X is saying; therefore, we must disapprove of Y. Instead of reacting to what X is saying, we react to X personally. Of course, such a line of thought is unfair: X's personality and X's actions are not necessarily relevant to what X is saying. Even a scoundrel can have a good idea. This process is a variation of the principle of transfer described in the chapter on propaganda: we transfer our feelings about the person who is speaking to what that person is saying. For instance, let us say that former president Nixon were to make some statement about foreign policy. If we were to say that Nixon's statement was worthless because Nixon behaved reprehensibly in the Watergate affair, then we would be guilty of an abusive *ad hominem* argument against Nixon.

Sometimes a person's ideas are challenged or criticized because of a particular position that the person is in: "Mr. X, a member of the city council, is proposing that the roof of the Town Hall be reshingled. But Mr. X is in the reshingling business. Therefore, it's obvious that he's just hoping to get the contract for himself. Therefore, we shouldn't listen to his suggestion." Such a line of thought is unfair, and the reasons for challenging Mr. X's proposal are irrelevant. The roof may actually need to be reshingled. The speaker has judged Mr. X, not what Mr. X has suggested. This type of irrelevant appeal is called a **circumstantial ad hominem** argument.

Another type of ad hominem argument is **guilt by association.** A person is judged because of his associations, his friends, his family, not because of anything he has done: he frequents a certain club; his brother-in-law was an embezzler; his wife is a gossip; his son is a defector from the army; his daughter has an illegitimate child; he played golf with someone who has connections with organized crime. Again, what the person is saying is the issue, not who his associates are. If his associates are relevant to the issue, then that relevance should be established, not insinuated.

Another technique by which the personality of a speaker is sometimes discredited is called **poisoning the well.** An enemy, when he poisons a well, ruins the water; no matter how good or how pure that water was, it is now tainted and hence unusable. When an opponent uses this technique, he casts such aspersions on a person that that person cannot possibly recover and defend himself without making matters much worse:

> CITY COUNCILMAN: The Mayor's a very good talker. Yes, talk he can do . . . and do well. But when it comes time for action, that's a different matter.

How can the mayor respond? If he remains silent, he runs the risk of appearing to accept the councilman's criticisms. But if he stands up and defends himself, then he is talking; and the more he talks, the more he appears to be confirming the accusations. The well has been poisoned, and the mayor is in a difficult position.

A second type of irrelevance can be called **passing the buck.** There are at least two variations: the *tu quoque* argument and the *counter-question.*

Tu quoque is the Latin phrase for "you too." Jones says to Turner, "Don't criticize me for not getting my report in on time; you don't always get your reports in on time." That statement may be true, but it is irrelevant. The issue at hand is Jones' behavior, not Turner's. Turner's behavior is a separate issue. Furthermore, even if Turner is or has been equally guilty, his guilt does not justify Jones' behavior. Two wrongs do not make a right. The *tu quoque* fallacy is sometimes called **shifting the blame.**

The **counter-question** occurs when, instead of answering a specific question, the speaker poses another question. Taylor asks Forbes, "Can you give me one good reason to approve your request?" Forbes replies, "Can you give me one good reason not to approve it?" The second question may have some relevance, but not at that time. Before the second speaker asks that counter-question, he is obliged to answer the first question. Often he can't and is merely trying to camouflage the weakness of his position.

Then there is the **irrelevant reason.** A group of people are discussing Topic X. Gradually the specific nature of Topic X becomes blurred; reasons are offered and supporting evidence is cited, but these reasons and this evidence address themselves not to Topic X but to some other topic, one perhaps related to X. For instance, some people are discussing whether to approve a new taxation proposal. "Yes, we should," claims one person. "The present tax system is too complicated; it is too hard to understand, and it is too confusing." Note that this person's arguments are irrelevant. They have nothing to do with the proposal under discussion. They address themselves to some weakness in the old program. The complexity of the present tax system is a separate issue. If it's too complex, then discussion should focus upon ways of simplifying it. But the complexity of the present system is no reason for adopting the new system.

Always make certain that the evidence supports the specific issue, not some related issue.

A variation of the irrelevant reason is the **non sequitur,** a Latin phrase that translates "it does not follow." A *non sequitur* is a statement that claims to make a cause and effect relationship when, in fact, there is no logical connection between the premises and the conclusion. Examine the following argument: A celebrity comments in a commercial, "Folks, you may not realize it, but I still get very nervous when I have to go on camera. Therefore, it's very important that I look my best. When those cameras come in for a close-up, my teeth have to be as white as possible. Therefore, I use Pepomint. Pepomint makes my teeth white." The conclusion here is a *non sequitur:* Having white teeth has nothing to do with being nervous before a camera.

Then, if this celebrity should use this particular argument to persuade you to buy Pepomint, he would have a second non sequitur. His argument would be something like this: "Whenever you go on camera, you want to make certain that your teeth are as white as they can be. I have found that Pepomint works for me. If it works for me, it will work for you. Therefore, if you want white teeth for those close-ups, buy Pepomint." Strictly speaking, the celebrity is addressing only those people who have to face close-up shots on camera. Now, of course, we realize that this is not what the commercial intends, but this is indeed what the commercial says.

The use of the **irrelevant** and the **selected detail** has already been described in the chapter entitled Suggestion. Here is another example from a leading national magazine of using irrelevant, selected details. The European Human-Rights Court is investigating the practice of corporal punishment—specifically, the birching of males between the age of fourteen and twenty on the Isle of Man. The article describes the reaction of the people to this investigation, and the opening paragraph reads as follows:

> On a freezing day, the protesters marched 4,000-strong on the Tynwald, one of the world's oldest parliaments, singing the national anthem and carrying placards that demanded: "Keep the Birch!" Led by a cigar-smoking housewife, a blind member of the Tynwald and a birching judge, it was the first major protest march that this quiet island of 60,000 people had seen in 30 years. "We are determined to keep the birch," insisted the housewife, Peggy Irving. "Our entire future is at stake."

This is spicy, colorful, and entertaining writing, but it is irresponsible and unprofessional news reporting. It would be very difficult for a reader to get through that first paragraph without forming a judgment about the people. We picture the cigar-smoking woman and the blind parliament member, and we are tempted to chuckle. We note Peggy Irving's overstatement and we chuckle again. The writer of the article has manipulated our attitude here rather than allowed us to formulate our own attitude. The words *cigar-smoking, blind,* and *birching* are irrelevant—and Mrs. Irving's statement is a selective one: The writer could have found other statements that would have created an entirely different impression. Furthermore, the article was introduced by referring to the investigation "into one of the most hallowed Manx traditions—'birching,' the custom of flogging youthful lawbreakers." Note the word *youthful,* as opposed to *young* or *adolescent* or *teen-age,* a word that carries a connotation of innocence, playfulness, and caprice. Note that the fact that only males are birched is omitted in that introduction. Note also the word *hallowed,* a word consciously selected, a word that gives the impression that the people regard their right to inflict corporal punishment as something sacred and holy, and hence that gives the impression that these people are a bunch of fanatics.

Note also that all the facts that the article relates are probably true. In this context, however, many of the facts are irrelevant. These irrelevant details create a bias against the people of the Isle of Man. Unfortunately, the judgments that this article invites are effected not by the reader but by the writer. A different writer might have effected a completely opposite judgment had he selected different details.

Now, writers have every right to try to effect a judgment or an attitude. But this right is predicated on the writer's responsibility to speak his mind openly, not through insinuation, and to give reasons for his point of view. Merely to insert that point of view as if it were fact is irresponsible writing.

Another type of irrelevance is the **argumentum ad baculum,** or **appeal to force.** A judge says to a witness, "If you don't cooperate, you will be held in contempt of court." The use of pressure or force may sometimes be useful, but it does not constitute a good reason for doing something. Being held in contempt of court is not a good reason for cooperating; it is merely a description of what will happen if the witness doesn't cooperate. The *argumentum ad baculum,* in effect, says that the person who has the power is by definition right. Blackmailers use the *argumentum ad baculum;* so do all people who say, "Do it my way or else!"

The **appeal to ignorance (argumentum ad ignorantiam)** is still another irrelevant appeal. This appeal takes different shapes: "You can't prove your claim; therefore, your claim is false." "You can't disprove what I say; therefore, my claim is right." For instance, "No one has ever been able to prove that God exists; therefore, He does not exist." "You haven't been able to give me one specific example that there is corruption in City Hall; therefore, your claim is false. There is no corruption."

Needless to say, one should not accept premises without proof. But what is important to realize is that the absence of proof does not necessarily mean that the premise is false; it merely means that there is no proof to substantiate that premise. My not being able to cite a specific example of corruption in City Hall does not mean that there is no corruption; it merely means that I can't think of an example. I may have read a list of scandals in the newspaper two weeks ago without having committed to memory any of the details.

Just because you can't prove something does not mean that your claim is automatically false. The weakness may be with you, not with your claim.

IRRELEVANT AUTHORITY

The next set of irrelevant appeals fall into a broad class called **appeal to authority (argumentum ad verecundiam)**. A statement or opinion of some outside source is often referred to in order to strengthen an argument. The statement or opinion of that outside source, however, may not be relevant to the specific issue at hand. People may not realize the irrelevance, however, and they may allow this false or irrelevant or improper authority to influence their beliefs. The appeal to authority takes many shapes: **he said it (ipse dixit)**. This is a variation of the testimonial device mentioned in the chapter on propaganda. A popular or prestigious person or someone with impressive titles or credentials is cited to give support to an idea or argument. But sometimes the person quoted is speaking outside his area of expertise; hence, his opinion should carry no more weight than that of anyone else. Few listeners, however, are likely to notice the irrelevance. They may transfer their positive feelings for the impressive person to what the person is saying. For instance, "We need penal reform and we need it immediately. Our prisons are places in which the God-given dignity of man is plundered. In fact, that great humanitarian, Albert Schweitzer, said, 'As long as one person is denied his essential rights and dignities as a human being, no one is free.' Given the present conditions, ladies and gentlemen, neither you nor I am free."

There is much that could be challenged in the passage just quoted. For now, let's examine the allusion to Schweitzer. He may have been a great humanitarian; he may have made the statement, and the statement may indeed be a noble one, but his statement is irrelevant to the issue at hand. First, Schweitzer had no expertise in penology. Second, his statement is general and idealistic, but it has nothing to do with prison systems: Schweitzer is being quoted out of context. His statement is being asked to mean something it was never intended to mean.

Just because an important person says something does not make that statement either true or relevant.

The Schweitzer example suggests another type of *ipse dixit* argument: the **appeal to the past** or to some **past authority.** The Bible, a quotation from Washington or Lincoln or Martin Luther King, Jr. or John F. Kennedy, a line from Shakespeare, a remark from Plato or Aristotle is used to support an idea. Such sources are often irrelevant and, like the Schweitzer quotation, are frequently quoted out of context. You can find an authority from the past—including the Bible—to support just about any position that you want to support. Such references should not be regarded as proof or evidence.

Because something is in print or because someone important said it is no reason to accept it. Before you accept any statement as authorative evidence or proof, you must first establish its context and its relevance.

Then there is the **vague appeal to authority:** "Doctors say . . ." "A leading medical institution says . . ." "Laboratory experiments at a leading university say . . ." "I read in the newspaper that . . ." "I heard on the radio that . . ." "I heard that . . ." "They say that . . ." "I read somewhere that . . ." When statements such as these are presented as evidence, they should be challenged or ignored unless much more specific data accompany them. The statements may be sound, but you should not automatically accept them as fact or evidence unless you investigate them further.

Apriority is another type of false authority. When you argue *a priori,* you argue from theory. You regard what you suspect to be true as if it were true. Common lead-in phrases are "I'm sure that . . ." "I just know that . . ." "My experience tells me that . . . will happen." Example: You and a friend are driving in a section of the country that neither of you has visited before. The gas gauge reads almost empty. You say to your companion, "Listen, we'd better get off this road and find out where a gas station is." Your companion replies, "Oh, don't worry. I'm sure that there's a gas station on this road." The fact is, your friend is not sure. He merely suspects or hopes. His past driving experience suggests that all major roads have gas stations at appropriate intervals. Or he may have noted that there have been gas stations on this road every twenty miles or so. Regardless, he can't be sure that there is a gas station on that road.

The *a priori* argument is like the emotional appeal of trust or hope. But it is a form of false authority. Unless a person has concrete evidence to support his claim, he cannot be sure and he cannot know. And, while experience may be of value to guide us in making inferences and decisions, it is rarely reliable when it is the only guide. Even an educated guess is still a guess.

Closely related to apriority is the **appeal to faith.** "Listen, I know what I'm doing. You've got to have faith in me. Just trust me." If you do go along with the speaker because of such an appeal, remember that you're taking a risk. Things may indeed turn out well, but there is no guarantee that they will.

Then there are appeals to what can be called the **sacred cow.** These are ideas that we hold dear: justice, freedom, democracy, the law, religion. When a person says that because you challenge his statement, you also challenge one of these ideas, he is using an irrelevant appeal to a sacred cow. "What do you mean by criticizing what the preacher said this morning? Are you against religion?" "When you criticize the President, you criticize all that he stands for: democracy, the American way of life." Such a line of thought is nonsense. Your attacking a person's statement does not mean that you are attacking either the person or the ideals he stands for.

Minority groups—religious, ethnical, racial, or ad hoc pressure groups—sometimes use this appeal. "I know why you're disagreeing with me; you're just antifeminist." "You know as well as I do that there is a strong feeling against Moravians in this community. The reason that Peter got such a stiff sentence for attempted robbery is that he's a Moravian." This appeal is a variation of the *ad hominem* argument mentioned earlier. It is often—perhaps usually—simply not relevant.

Aphorisms, clichés, slogans, proverbs, platitudes are sometimes used as authority to convince or persuade. For instance, the saying "Where there's a will, there's a way" becomes a substitute for hard thinking and offers only glib encouragement. A husband responds to a wife who wants to go shopping: "Remember, dear, a fool and his money are soon parted." "Love thy neighbor" is cited to criticize a government's military activities. "The only thing we have to fear is fear itself" is used to cajole a person into doing something about which he has apprehensions. Such sayings are irrelevant; they provide no authority for the specific issue at hand; they merely oversimplify. Furthermore, for every adage offered to support an argument, another adage can be found to express the opposite point of view. The wife could respond to her husband by claiming, "You can't take it with you." The person who has apprehensions could reply "Fools rush in where angels fear to tread." And a person who supports the government's military activities can just as easily use the old saying "It is noble and proper to die for one's country." Such use of familiar sayings offers neither proof nor evidence, nor do they even strengthen an argument. More often than not, they merely confuse the issue.

Sometimes **jargon** is used to give the impression of authority. "Dial, with hexachlorophine!" But what is hexachlorophine and why does it make Dial better than any other soap? The fancy word "hexachlorophine" is used to impress us. If we're impressed with the fancy word, we may transfer our positive reaction to the product itself and buy it. A politician makes the following statement: "We have moved from a hyper-inflated, supersaturated utilization of resources and, by controlling our cost overhead by judicious anti-inflationary measures, have reached a near total zero-deficit operating budget, including both inter-cameral and extra-cameral considerations." This may sound impressive to some people, but the words don't mean a thing. Always be leery of pompous jargon; it often camouflages both content and thought—at least hard thought.

People sometimes use an **appeal to tradition or precedent:** "We've always done it this way; therefore, why change?" "We've never done it this way before, so why should we start now?" Such statements in and of themselves should be allowed little weight and authority. There should be better reasons than just tradition or precedent to determine a course of action. Circumstances change with time; what may have been an appropriate way of doing things five years ago is not necessarily an appropriate way now. Tradition and precedent should be respected but not idolized.

The **etymology** of a word is occasionally cited to support a position. Let us say that an atheist is trying to muster support for his view. "Listen," he insists, "you claim that religion is based upon love. I disagree. Love is not the basis of religion. Religion is based upon control and fear. Look at the very words that we use. The word *reverence* comes from the Latin word *vereor,* a word that means 'fear.' The relationship of man to God is fear, not love. And even the word *religion* itself comes from the Latin *religo,* a verb that means 'to bind' or 'to fetter.' Religion ties man down; it tries to control him; it shackles and enslaves. Nowhere is love even suggested." The fallacy here is that the meaning of words change. The etymology of a word does not necessarily constitute any evidence about how the word is now being used. A word is important, not for what it once meant, but for what it means now.

APPEAL TO NUMBERS

Numbers can indicate splendid precision. Ironically, those very numbers can be used to mislead and even to deceive. A number or a statistic means absolutely nothing in a vacuum. In order for a number or a statistic to have any meaning and any relevance, it must be accompanied by a context.

If we're dealing with a statistic, we should ascertain who gathered the statistic, what process was used, how many people were polled, how these people were selected, what specific questions were asked, how these questions were phrased, and whether either the interviewer or the questions used any of the techniques described in the chapter on suggestion.

First, let's examine different ways of describing and manipulating a series of numbers. A small business, let us say, has eleven employees, who make the following annual salaries:

1—$6,000	6—$12,000
2—$6,000	7—$23,000
3—$7,000	8—$24,000
4—$8,000	9—$24,000
5—$8,000	10—$24,000
	11—$25,000

The company could add all the salaries, divide by eleven, and have the figure of $15,181. They could then call this figure the average. Such an average is called a *mean average.* Note that such a figure is both deceptive and worthless in this context. No one in the business makes $15,000, and most people make either considerably more or considerably less.

The mean average should be accompanied by two other averages, the *mode* and the *median*. The mode is the most frequent number or numbers among a series of figures. In the above example, there are actually two modes—most people make either around $7,000 or around $24,000. The mode is often a much more valuable and relevant figure than the mean.

The median is the number that is in the middle of the series of numbers when those numbers are arranged from highest to lowest or lowest to highest. The median in the above series is $12,000; it's not a particularly useful number but it does help us to establish the context of the averages.

There are two other methods to help establish the context of a figure, the *range* and the *frequency distribution*. The range in the above example is $19,000, from $6,000 to $25,000; the frequency distribution tells us that two people make $6,000, that one makes $7,000, that two make $8,000, that one makes $12,000, that one makes $23,000, that three make $24,000, and that one makes $25,000.

A common fallacy occurs when the mean average is interpreted as the mode. "What a wonderful company," someone might remark, "where the average salary is so high." Nonsense! you should think, unless you know that the word *average* is referring to the mode and not the mean.

When dealing with the word *average*, therefore, it is essential to distinguish between mean and mode; and so much the better if you can ascertain the median, the frequency distribution, and the range.

Percentages can also be misleading. "During Mayor Cord's administration, corruption has decreased by fifty percent," claims a supporter for Mayor Cord. That claim may be true; but there may now be only two crooks instead of four—not a very significant difference. The percentage, however, sounds much more impressive than the figures. One can make the percentages look even more impressive: "During the previous administration, instances of corruption were two hundred percent higher than they have been under the present administration." Two hundred percent sounds quite impressive. In fact, there isn't much of a difference in corruption between the two administrations.

Then there are **misleading sampling techniques.** "Sixty percent

of the people want McCormick." This may be true, but the poll
may have been taken in a heavily Republican district, most of
whose residents support the Republican candidate, McCormick.
This deception is an example of what can result from a **limited
sample.** The sample of people polled was not representative of the
total voting constituency.

Similar to the limited sample is the **small sample:** "Sixty percent
of the people want Miller." Again, the claim may be true, but only
thirty people were polled. Of those thirty, eighteen wanted Miller.
But thirty people is not enough to constitute a meaningful statistic.
Thirty people cannot be considered representative of the entire
voting population.

Then there are the **vague statistics:** "A recent survey shows that
more doctors prescribe Brand Z than any other brand for common
headaches." The words "a recent survey" can be concealing a great
deal, and these words should not be granted a stamp of authority
unless much more information is supplied. There is also the **misleading statistic:** "A recent survey shows that more people prefer
Brand Z than any other brand." Perhaps true. But look at the following data:

> 85 people preferred Brand A.
> 80 people preferred Brand B.
> 89 people preferred Brand C.
> 91 people preferred Brand Z.

The total number of people polled was 345. Of this 345, 91 people,
or under 30 percent, preferred Brand Z. Brand Z is not capturing a
significantly larger share of the market than any other brand, although it is true that more people prefer Brand Z over any other
brand.

Finally, there is the **appeal to large numbers,** a variation of the
bandwagon device. "Everyone is doing X; therefore, do X." "Four
million Americans can't be wrong." A large number may be cited
to try to impress us. We should not necessarily be impressed. Even
if forty million people are doing X or buying Z, that is no reason for
our doing X or for our buying Z. The fact that a lot of people are
doing something is irrelevant unless much better arguments are
available.

CONFIDENT SPECULATION

ALTHOUGH EACH OF us knows many other categories of irrelevance that we might cite here, let's look at one more—a distant cousin of the appeal to authority. When people make assertions that are speculative but that are expressed as if they were fact, the phenomenon is called **confident speculation**. For instance, there are **personal assurances:** "I'm sure that . . ." "I just know that . . ." "I have every reason to believe that . . ." I am confident that . . ."

This type of apriority offers assurances, but there can be no guarantees for these assurances . . . unless the being making them is God.

A subcategory is the **appeal to personal experience:** "From my experience I have learned that . . ." "From my experience I know that . . ." "I knew someone who . . ." This form of apriority also offers assurances as if they were facts, but the reasons to support these assurances are unreliable. A person's experiences are worth hearing about and worth considering; personal experiences can offer guidelines, but they do not in and of themselves constitute a criterion for accepting a position.

Sometimes the **Domino Theory** is offered as evidence: "If we do A, then B will happen. If B happens, then C will happen. And if C happens, D will happen." Indeed, there are times when we can with some accuracy predict the future. If we blow up the dam, the water will indeed flood the valley below. But far too often a person will try to predict a less clear-cut sequence of events. Many a person uses the word "will" when he should have said "may." "Unless we ratify this contract, our employees will strike." Well, maybe they will and maybe they won't. The statement is unreliable as evidence. The speaker has confused speculation with fact: There may be a high degree of probability behind that speculation; nonetheless, it is still speculation: It is not necessarily fact.

Finally, there is an **appeal to omniscience.** This occurs when people speculate about what might have happened if something else had or had not happened: "If only Kennedy had not been assassinated, he would have been able to bring the war in Vietnam to a much quicker end; if the war had ended sooner, we would not have had such hostility toward the government; if there had not been such hostility toward the government, we wouldn't have had the radical youth movements of the late 60s; and if we hadn't had such radical youth movements, we wouldn't have the general disdain for authority that now characterizes this country." The speaker here may be guilty of arrant oversimplification, but he is also guilty of **confusing speculation with fact.** It is fine to speculate, but none of us are sufficiently omniscient to say what *would* have happened.

All too often such arguments are used to rationalize our own failures: "If I hadn't stayed up late, I would have been more alert; if I had been more alert, I would have made a better impression; if I had made a better impression, I would have gotten the job." Again, speculation should not be granted the stamp of truth.

This chapter has cited a number of irrelevant appeals. Since rarely is there a discussion in which there is not some irrelevance—some discussions run rampant with irrelevance—it is important to be alert to it and not let it persuade us. The reasons that irrelevance often looms so large are complex, but certainly one of the reasons is that those who would be convincing often are not objective and will use any arguments they can think of to support their beliefs or positions or attitudes. Furthermore, these beliefs and attitudes often have not been consciously formulated; hence, these people often do not have very good reasons for them. "I know what I like; don't confuse me with the facts" is not glaring overstatement in characterizing the attitudes of many people with whom we all must deal.

Diversion

*Ridicule is often the only weapon re-
maining to conscious inferiority.*
F. H. Cowles, *Gaius Verres: An
Historical Study*

Diversions occur intentionally and unintentionally. The diversion
can be a useful tool when arguments fail you, when you are backed
into a corner, when you feel that you are losing or are about to lose,
or when you feel uncomfortable with the drift of a conversation.
On the other hand, diversion can be used against you if you're not
alert. It is just as easy to be distracted as it is to distract.

Distraction occurs when emotionalism enters a discussion; it
occurs when irrelevancies are admitted in, since most diversionary
factors are irrelevancies. Hence, many of the devices cited in earlier chapters can lead to diversions. For instance, if someone poses
a counter-question and if you pick up the bait and pursue that
counter-question, you are off the topic and onto a diversion, away
from the original question. If irrelevant details enter an issue and if
those details are challenged, then the discussion may get sidetracked; unfortunately, if those details are not challenged, the audience may become biased. When an *ad hominem* argument is
used, the issue becomes sidetracked to the personality of the
speaker rather than to what the speaker is actually saying.

Needless to say, a reasoned argument or discussion is one that
avoids digressions or diversions. The aim of this chapter is not to
supply suggestions but rather to furnish cautions. If you recognize
the tricks and pitfalls, you may be able to avoid being tricked.

There are two prime sources of diversion: the red herring and the straw man.

THE RED HERRING

To divert hounds from pursuing a scent, a herring would be dragged across their path. The hounds, distracted by this new scent, would follow the scent of the herring and would forget about their original goal. From this practice comes the expression "a red herring." A red herring is a detail or remark inserted into a discussion, either intentionally or unintentionally, that sidetracks the discussion. The red herring is invariably irrelevant and is often emotionally charged. The participants in the discussion go after the red herring and forget what they were initially talking about; in fact, they may never get back to their original topic.

Observe the dynamics of the following dialogue. Betty and Philip are deep into a discussion about forced bussing.

> BETTY: But you say that bussing will relieve racial tension and will improve the quality of education. I don't see how. If children are herded onto busses and shipped out miles from their homes, they will merely resent the inconvenience, and tension will become even worse.
>
> PHILIP: Yes, that may be true for a while. But eventually these kids will get to know each other, and when that happens, many of the barriers that now exist will be broken.
>
> BETTY: That's dumb! How can you make a statement like that! Who are you to predict the future! You're just babbling idealistic rubbish. It's you idealists who are responsible for so many of the problems that now beset the world.
>
> PHILIP: I beg your pardon! What are you talking about? Idealists have been responsible for most of the good that is present in the world. If we didn't have idealists, we wouldn't have had this country. Don't you think that idealism—the hope for a better way of life, the hope for personal freedom—was the prime motivation for the colonists' massive venture to leave England and to begin fresh?

BETTY: I do not! It seems to me that the one thing that the colonists did not believe in was personal freedom. Look at the Blue Laws. Look at the Salem witch trials. Do you call that personal freedom? It seems to me that the colonists had no commitment to personal freedom; in fact, just the opposite.

PHILIP: I disagree. Look at the Articles of Confederation. Look at the Boston Tea Party. Look at . . .

Whatever happened to forced bussing? Betty and Philip are miles from their original topic. They followed the red herring of idealism and then another red herring of the nature of freedom in the colonies. The chances of their getting back to the subject of forced bussing are slim.

The use of **humor, sarcasm, ridicule, innuendo, parody,** or a **bodily gesture** can lead to a diversion. These means can alter the course of a discussion by triggering an emotional reaction in the person against whom they are employed. That person becomes insulted and may gear his remarks to save face rather than to continue addressing the issue.

Another technique is the **witty remark.** The witty remark makes people laugh, and when people laugh, the tone of the discussion may be altered. Recall the incident that occurred when one of President Carter's chief aides was accused of spitting at a person in a Washington bar. A congressman, in a public speech ostensibly about the President, remarked that Carter's tenure had moved from "great expectations to great expectorations." Such cheap shots accomplish no good; rather, they distort the issue and discourage rational discussion.

A similar technique occurs when **a person interprets literally what was said figuratively.** Mr. Hunt is decrying the conditions in a certain part of town. "In fact," he remarks, "I would rather live in the depths of a jungle than in the squalor of that part of town," and he proceeds to show that the jungle, with all its native dangers and threats, is safer than that part of town. His opponent, Mr. Rand, then responds. Sandwiched in his remarks is something like this: "Of course, we can't take Mr. Hunt very seriously. After all, he wants to live in a jungle—and certainly he'd be much more comfortable dealing with snakes and mosquitoes than with the very real problems that we have to face." Mr. Rand's remarks are dirty. By taking a figure of speech and interpreting it literally, he tries to discredit Mr. Hunt. And if the audience laughs at Mr. Hunt, they will be less willing to take him seriously and listen to what he has to say.

Now, Mr. Rand could go even farther. He could play with his opponent's last name, "Hunt." He could go off on a diversion, showing how Mr. Hunt would indeed be better off hunting in some jungle. The audience might be highly amused; Mr. Hunt might be squirming. If, when Mr. Hunt regained the floor, he were so flustered that he argued badly, we would be witnessing still another diversionary tactic: Getting a person sufficiently upset so that he loses his wits and composure. If this occurred, Mr. Hunt would be playing right into Mr. Rand's hands. If Mr. Hunt loses his ability to think clearly, he may make foolish statements or he may behave badly and clumsily, thereby further weakening his position.

You can put an opponent on the defensive by speaking confidently, by using esoteric facts that your opponent may be afraid to challenge, by using technical jargon, by making your opponent afraid to admit his ignorance, by using such intimidating phrases as "Surely you know (agree/realize) that . . ." "Of course no one would disagree with me when I say that . . ." "Obviously . . ." and so on. If your opponent is at all unsure of himself, such confidence may fluster him. However, if he is sharp, he may call your bluff.

A diversion can occur when a person makes a **petty objection.** You make a slight mistake and your opponent pounces upon you for that mistake, even though the mistake is a minor one and even though the mistake does not alter by one jot the point that you have been making. What happens then is that you may become flustered, perhaps exasperated, and you may momentarily lose confidence in what you are saying. Your credibility may be weakened. People may assume that, because you were wrong on this one point, you are wrong in other areas. Such pettiness is sometimes called **nit-picking.**

For instance, you and a friend are arguing whether or not the government should institute an embargo upon Japanese automobiles. You, arguing for the proposition, make the point that previous embargoes have been effective, citing the example of Lincoln's embargo of 1860, and you describe the events of that act. Your friend then jumps upon you, claiming that the Lincoln embargo was not instituted until April 1861, and he makes a big fuss over your incorrect date. Now, it is true that your date was wrong; however, the fact is that your error makes no difference whatsoever to the soundness of your argument.

Let us continue the example. Suppose he allows your incorrect date to slip by but challenges you instead on the effectiveness of Lincoln's embargo, claiming that it was much less effective than you had realized. Let us say that he is right: The blockade was not effective. Regardless, you are both still off on a red herring. You have not moved one dash closer to determining whether the present proposed embargo is a good idea or not. And just because your friend has scored a point by weakening your appraisal of the 1861 embargo, neither of you should feel that he has scored a point toward the issue that you are arguing: the proposed embargo upon Japanese cars.

Sometimes a person will try to create a diversion by feigning ignorance; the speaker claims that he doesn't understand something that his opponent has said, i.e., he **plays dumb.** This technique may make the opponent look foolish. He may try to re-explain and get muddled; the audience may lose a bit of confidence in him and in his position. On the other hand, if he is sharp, he will come right back at the speaker and make him appear the fool.

THE STRAW MAN

When you take something your opponent has said, exaggerate or distort it, and then attack what you have exaggerated or distorted, you have created a straw man. You have misrepresented your opponent's statements, and then you have attacked not his statements but the misrepresentation of those statements.

A straw man can be created by **extending** an opponent's ideas: "You are advocating A; the next thing, you'll be advocating B, and then C, and then D." Then you show how terrible or foolish or impractical D is. Of course, your opponent never suggested D, but the audience may have forgotten that fact.

Sometimes, instead of extending your opponent's arguments, you **put words into his mouth.** You either imply or state that he said something that in fact he never said or that his words meant something that in fact he never intended them to mean. An opponent is arguing that police should have the right to force entry into a place when they know that that place is harboring a criminal. You then put forth a line of argument in which you create a picture of police indiscriminately entering private homes. "How can he advocate such a fundamental abuse of personal rights!" you exclaim. "How can he want a situation where the police can burst into private homes merely because they think that some criminal is there! He seems to want a police state—for surely there is little difference between what he is advocating and a police state." And you go on depicting the horrors of a police state.

Needless to say, your opponent did not suggest a police state. You are creating a straw man by attributing to him statements and intentions that he did not express.

You can create a straw man by **attacking an example.** In the process of making a point, your opponent uses an example or an illustration or an analogy. You then attack that illustration. You assume that because you have weakened his illustration, you have also weakened his argument. If he lets you get away with this, he may deserve to be discredited. He should realize that just because an example is weak, his argument or his position is not necessarily weak. The fault may be with the example, not with his position. This device is similar to the petty objection device cited earlier in this chapter, and it may be a variation of the twisting of the figurative into the literal device also cited earlier.

A speaker can create a straw man by **attacking the alternative.** For instance, X is the issue being discussed. A speaker finds that he cannot defend X very well; perhaps he can't think of arguments; perhaps X is itself a weak position. Regardless, instead of addressing his comments to the specific issue, the speaker creates a straw man by discussing the alternatives to X and he then goes after those alternatives. The issue at hand might be whether the compulsory athletic program at a particular school should be continued. A speaker supports the idea of compulsory athletics but perhaps cannot think of good arguments to support his position. Therefore, he examines the alternatives: "What will happen if athletics are not compulsory? The kids will have too much free time and will get into trouble. Also, there may not be enough bodies to field our athletic squads." Now, these are not sound reasons for supporting compulsory athletics.

A variation occurs in this example: Harriet says to Sam, "You shouldn't be so careless with your rifle; you could get killed." Sam replies, "I could just as easily get killed crossing the street." Sam's statement may be true, but it is irrelevant. Shifting to another problem proves nothing.

Above all, the straw man is a misrepresentation and distortion. The witty or cute remark can create a straw man. Mr. Rand, in the example cited earlier in this chapter, created a straw man when he caricatured Mr. Hunt. In interpreting literally what Hunt said figuratively, he turned Hunt's comments into a joke and tried to make Hunt look like a fool.

You can create a straw man by oversimplifying your opponent's arguments and reducing them to an absurdity.

Or you can create a straw man by attacking your opponent's weakest argument while ignoring his stronger arguments.

The following letter to the editor of *TV Guide* is almost a textbook example of straw man techniques. The letter responds to an article that described how the Nielsen television rating company approximates the number of people watching a particular television program. "Nielsen statisticians pick random locations [of 1170 TV homes] from a Census Bureau master list and make sure they are spread geographically across the country." Not all of these 1170 homes are counted each week. "Thus, on a typical ratings day last winter, Nielsen reported viewing information from about 993 homes." The response:

> Now we know how to placate the masses and, at the same time, bypass the whole democratic structure altogether. Isn't it delightful to realize that the viewing tastes of some 200 million individuals need not concern one, since those tastes are in the control of a very small group of people. What a simple solution we have been offered! Perhaps our next President can be selected by sampling the desires of 1170 families (although 993 will do in a pinch), and those families will resolve that pressing problem without disturb-

ing the rest of us. Think of the tremendous savings in time
and energy not to mention costs. Why, the mind boggles at
the infinite and exciting possibilities. Is this system a fair
representation of the feelings of all?

It is not incumbent upon you or me to take a position on the
effectiveness of the Nielsen rating system, but the reply clearly
illustrates the straw-man technique. Of course, the letter has a
point to make, but that point seems to get lost because of the
presentation. Who can take seriously a letter that relies upon misrepresentation, extension of an idea to the point of absurdity, and
overall distortion?

When a discussion has gone on for a while, both participants
and listeners may become fatigued. They may at least temporarily
forget just what the precise topic is and may allow diversions to
enter that discussion without even realizing that they have lost the
track. They may not notice that they are following a red herring or
that they are discussing a straw man, not the specific issue. They
may confuse what *appears* to be relevant with what *is* relevant.
The next chapter will show how irrelevancies and diversions oper-
ate in a discussion.

Interlude: A Discussion

The newspapers! Sir, they are the most villainous—licen-
tious—abominable—infernal—not that I ever read them—
no—I make it a rule never to look into a newspaper.
Sheridan, The Critic, I, i

The setting is a faculty meeting at the Lincoln School, a private, secondary boarding school. The faculty is responding to a proposal that each student be required to participate in a team sport during at least one of the three seasons each year: fall, winter, or spring. The present athletic policy requires only that each student participate in some form of supervised athletic activity.

Mr. ANDREWS: I think that the idea is a good one. It seems to me that these kids do not get enough exercise. They're at a time in their life when exercise is imperative. If this school is going to be responsible to the whole student, then we have to do everything we can to nourish both the mind and the body.

Mr. BRAND: I agree. Look at Herb. He's thirty pounds overweight and, as far as I can tell, he doesn't do anything with his body. He attends classes and then goes to his dormitory and sits in front of the television. The only nourishment his body gets is from all the junk food that he eats. If we as a school allow this to happen, then we are indeed acting irresponsibly, just as Mr. Andrews says.

Mrs. CANNARD: Wait a minute, that's not fair. Herb has some specific glandular problems that account for his being overweight. Haven't you bothered to read his medical report—it's all there in black-and-white in his folder in the dean's office. You ought to do your homework before you make such statements.

MRS. DAVIS: That may be, but Mr. Brand's point is a good one. Besides, you can't expect us to read the folders of every kid in the school: there are over a thousand students. And, even if we were to read the medical records, what would that prove! The school's physical examination is just a perfunctory one—it takes about five minutes. Surely, a five minute examination doesn't tell us very much.

MRS. ELIOT: That may be, but let's get back to the topic. We're talking about required team sports. Now, you know how this school works. If we require all our students to join a team sport, the coaches will start getting greedy, and before you know it we'll be requiring kids to take a team sport for two terms and then for three terms. Every day at two P.M. all the kids will go rushing to the gym. What will happen to the debating team, the dramatics society, the science club? Those activities are just as important as team sports. In fact, I don't think we should be talking about team sports. We should be talking about requiring every student to participate in at least one extracurricular activity.

MR. FORD: What, are you against team sports! Let me tell you: I was required to play football when I was in school, and it was the best thing that ever happened to me. I hated it for a while, but eventually I got to understand the game and I ended up loving it—in fact, I played varsity football in college. Sometimes kids don't know what's good for them, and it's our job as professionals to guide them in their decision.

MRS. GREEN: That's right. We don't give them carte blanche in selecting their courses. We say that certain areas are important—English, math, history, a foreign language, a science, and so on—and we require them to take those courses. The same with athletics. We don't want to cater to instant gratification as the schools did in the late sixties, when the schools let them do whatever they wanted. Look at the trouble the schools got into then: riots, violence, kids who couldn't read or write. No, sir, I certainly don't want to go back to those days.

Mrs. Harris: Yes, indeed, those were awful days; I remember the violence all too well, and I'm glad that Mrs. Green mentioned it, because if we deplore violence, how can we permit football? Three students are walking around on crutches now just because of football. And do you remember Jimmy Doe—two years ago he broke his leg so badly that he'll always have to walk with a limp. We certainly weren't very responsible in his case. Sometimes I think that these coaches won't be satisfied until they see the whole school walking on crutches or until someone gets killed. Is that what we're waiting for? Is that what it's going to take to bring us to our senses?

This discussion could go on for hours and continue to be as unproductive as it so far has been. The participants are getting nowhere. The specific topic is being ignored, and the drift of the discussion is entirely desultory.

The reason that the discussion is so badly floundering is that the participants have not identified the issues. In order to discuss the topic productively, they must identify and evaluate certain questions. First, what type of athletic program is desirable? What does the school want its athletic program to do? If the participants cannot answer these questions, then they had better discontinue the argument. Second, to what extent does the present athletic program meet the school's goals? If it can be shown that the present program does indeed meet those goals, there is no need for further discussion. Third, is there anything in the present program that prevents the meeting of those goals? Fourth, if there is something in the present program that prevents the meeting of those goals, how serious is it? Can the present program be modified in order to meet the goals? Or is there something inherently unsatisfactory about the present program—so unsatisfactory that it warrants scrapping the program and coming up with a new program? Fifth, how and to what extent will the proposed idea meet those goals? Sixth, what undesirable consequences might result if the proposed idea were put into effect?

Unless the participants of the discussion can identify and answer these questions, they will probably continue to babble; the participants will become frustrated; the meeting will break up, and there will be no resolution. It is in situations such as these that the role of a chairman is so crucial. A good chairman will insist that the issues be identified and that people direct their remarks to the issues. He is like the steersman of a ship, who must know not only what course to take but also how to keep to that course; he must recognize adverse wind conditions that threaten his course, and he must be able to evaluate just how much he should yield to those conditions; but above all, he must know what his destination is and how to reach that destination. In the same way, any group trying to reach some conclusion must have at least one person who keeps the goals clearly in mind and who understands what steps are necessary to reach those goals.

The goal of the discussion that began this chapter is simply this: to determine whether the Lincoln School should require all of its students to participate in one team sport a year. Note that none of the participants of the discussion has directed his or her remarks toward that specific issue. They have talked about exercise in general, about violence in sports, about the value of football, and about the value of extracurricular activities. None of these is relevant, however, even though each is important to at least one of the participants. Let us look briefly at the dynamics of the discussion:

MR. ANDREWS: All he has to say is that students of high school age should have exercise. He says nothing about the present athletic program and nothing about the proposed program, but he likes the proposal. There is most likely some hidden agendum here, since he makes no attempt to specify why he likes the proposal.

MR. BRAND: His use of Herb is a type of straw man. Herb is an unusual example. One should ask Mr. Brand at least two questions: Why doesn't he assume some personal responsibility in getting Herb away from the television? And how would requiring Herb to join a team sport once a year remove the problem that Brand is describing? Brand seems to suggest that requiring the student to be on a team during one term each year is going to help remedy Herb's problems, but he offers not one reason for that belief.

MRS. CANNARD: She creates a diversion by attacking Brand's illustration. True, Brand's illustration was irrelevant, but there at least was a point: that the school is being irresponsible by allowing Herb to waste his time watching television. Mrs. Cannard apparently cannot see this point.

MRS. DAVIS: Things now go from bad to worse. Mrs. Davis is off on the red herring introduced by Mrs. Cannard. The school's medical examination is not the issue.

MRS. ELIOT tries to bring the discussion back to the issue, but her own hobbyhorse prevents her from remembering just what that issue is. She creates a straw man by extending the arguments of the original proposal; she speculates on what will happen when participation in team sports is required during each of the three seasons. Apparently, however, what's really on her mind is her favorite hobbyhorse, school activities, and she sees any tightening in the school's athletic program as a threat to those activities. One can easily imagine Mrs. Eliot riding her favorite hobbyhorse—required activities—whenever the chance arises.

MR. FORD seems obtuse enough to take Mrs. Eliot literally. Actually, he has his own hobbyhorse—the glories of football—and he is merely using Mrs. Eliot's remarks as a catalyst to mount his own horse. He seems to feel that whatever was good for him is good for everyone else.

MRS. GREEN has not been listening to the drift of the previous speakers, but she has picked up Ford's last words, and off she goes upon her own hobbyhorse. She seems to be motivated by fear, and this fear drives her to oversimplification.

MRS. HARRIS takes the discussion even farther off course. She generalizes from a few specific incidents, and out of those specific incidents she creates a lurid straw man.

We'll never know whether or not the Lincoln School changed its athletic requirement. If it did, it was probably done by executive fiat rather than by consensus, for consensus seems impossible.

One might say that the presentation of this discussion is itself a straw man, that no group of people is as inept as this group. Unfortunately, this group is not atypical. The dynamics of this discussion characterize many groups of people who do not listen carefully to each other and who are easily sidetracked. The participants find it difficult to distinguish between the relevant and the irrelevant. They often do not think clearly before they speak. Their remarks often indicate a hidden agendum that is not articulated; hence, they will use a discussion as an arena to ride their favorite hobbyhorses and to vent their pet peeves, and they will have difficulty subordinating their own concerns to the specific issue under consideration.

11

Ambiguity and Inference

How finely we argue upon mistaken facts!
Sterne, *Tristram Shandy*, IV, xxvii

This chapter and the following overlap a bit, since common to this chapter on ambiguity and to the next chapter on confusion is the problem and danger of making inferences. A person is faced with a choice in how to interpret a word or statement or an act or an utterance; perhaps he doesn't even consciously realize that there is a choice; regardless, he makes a decision quickly or without sufficient analysis or without clearly identifying the alternatives or without having complete information. At this point, he may have made an error in judgment, and this error will probably impair his effectiveness in pursuing whatever he is doing.

Verbal Ambiguity occurs when one uses a word or phrase that has two or more possible meanings or interpretations or when there is an event that can have more than one interpretation. A person may not realize that more than one interpretation is possible, or he may arbitrarily have to select one of the possible choices. He does select one at the exclusion of the others, and problems arise because of the exclusion. The ambiguity itself is not usually the problem. It is either the failure to recognize the ambiguity or the wrong choice that is the problem. An ambiguity usually requires a person to make an inference, and inferences are often either incorrect or incomplete. Inferences are often the result of misinterpretation.

Whenever an utterance allows more than one level of meaning, whenever an utterance implies more than it states, or whenever an utterance reflects a belief or attitude that is not specifically articulated, ambiguity is possible. Hence, several of the topics mentioned in Chapter 6, the chapter on suggestibility, can contribute to ambiguity. Take the metaphor, for instance. If I make a careless statement, unintentionally using a metaphor, and if you interpret my statement more precisely than I uttered it, ambiguity can occur. You ask me what I know about Ted Steele. "He's a bum," I reply. I may be using the word *bum* loosely, figuratively, merely to express my dislike for Steele. But you may interpret the word literally and picture Steele as an idle loafer.

A metaphor, since it invariably implies more than it states, invites a person to make an inference, and this inference may contribute to ambiguity. Suppose I make the following statement: "Marion became intoxicated when she heard that she had won the lottery." How should you interpret the word *intoxicated?* Did Marion become drunk? or was she intoxicated with delight?

Ambiguity can occur when the figurative use of a word is ignored. One of the Ten Commandments states, "Thou shalt not covet thy neighbor's wife." At least three words are used figuratively. *Covet* literally means to "lust after" or to "desire eagerly," but in context it really means to "have sexual dealings with" as well as to "lust after." Taking the commandment literally would sanction sleeping with a married person, as long as there was no intense desire or lust—obviously a distortion. *Neighbor* literally means "one who lives nearby," but in context it really means "all other human beings." Taking the commandment literally would sanction having sex with a married person as long as that person wasn't married to someone who lived nearby—obviously a distortion. *Wife* literally means a "married woman," but in context it really means a "married person." Taking the commandment literally would sanction a woman's having sex with any married man, since the commandment says nothing about thy neighbor's husband—obviously a distortion.

Take this example: Willy has borrowed the family car; as he is backing into a parking place, he hits a parking meter, and the back fender is dented. His father asks, "Did you dent that fender?" "No!" replies Willy, saying to himself that *he* didn't dent the fender: the parking meter dented it. By taking his father's words literally, Willy can claim innocence—although we know, and Willy knows, that he is purposely twisting what his father said. His father's statement actually meant, "Are you responsible for that dent?" or "Do you know anything about that dent?" People frequently do not say *exactly* what they mean, and it is improper to interpret literally what was either uttered imprecisely or intended to be figurative.

Ambiguity of statement can result from imprecise language, from words that are vague or abstract or relative. "Laurie is nice." What does *nice* mean? "Andrew is rich." What does *rich* mean? "Judge Gardiner is competent?" Competent at what? At maintaining order in court? At putting witnesses at ease? At running an efficient trial? At understanding the law? "Kevin is short." Short in relation to what? How short? The use of imprecise words easily leads to confusion.

Similarly, ambiguity can result from imprecise phraseology. The statement "Kevin is shorter than James" invites the listener to picture two relatively short people, an inference that may be incorrect. Kevin may be 5' 10" and James 6' 1". The statement as uttered is true, but the phraseology is deceptive.

Ambiguity can occur when a person is not sure just what an utterance intends, i.e., when a person suspects that there is a hidden agendum behind the utterance. A wife says to her husband, "I hear that that new restaurant, *Le Fleur*, is very good. Marge and Bill were there last night, and Marge raved about the food; she said that the service was first-rate and that the prices were pretty reasonable, too." The wife is ostensibly making a statement of fact, but there is the distinct possibility that she is hinting so that her husband will invite her to *Le Fleur*. The words of her statement are not ambiguous, but the intention of her statement may be.

So far we have been dealing primarily with two types of ambiguity: verbal ambiguity and ambiguity of statement. Verbal ambiguity occurs when words have more than one possible meaning and when the speaker or writer does not specify exactly which of the possible meanings he desires. A statement is ambiguous when it does not state exactly what it intends to state. Let us now examine some other types of ambiguity.

Ambiguity of tone. A friend of mine has just come up with an ingenious solution to a complex problem. "You are a sly one!" I remark. I intend my comment to be complimentary and to suggest an attitude of approval. But the tone of my comment may be misinterpreted. Either my friend or some third party may infer that my attitude is one of disapproval.

Irony. When we speak ironically, we mean the opposite of what we actually say. A friend of mine, through a series of carefully planned but entirely honorable negotiations, has just managed to secure a business deal that he has been after for a long time. "You scoundrel!" I remark. My remark is ironic. Although the word *scoundrel* usually suggests a disapproving attitude, in this context I am expressing approval, perhaps even flattery and admiration. But if my friend does not recognize the irony, he may misinterpret my remark.

Determining the tone of a statement can be difficult when that statement appears in print. When a statement is spoken, it is much easier to ascertain the attitude of the speaker than when the statement is written. Note the following headline from *Time* magazine:

ALASKA'S LINE STARTS PIPING—AT LAST

Is the word *piping* merely intended to be cute? Or is there more to it? And what about the phrase *at last?* Does it express sarcasm, frustration, relief, enthusiasm? The reader can't be sure; yet, the reader is invited to make an inference.

Accent. This device has already been discussed in the suggestibility chapter. An ambiguity occurs when we are not sure which words in a sentence should be accented, and a distortion occurs when we accent the wrong word and hence change the meaning of the sentence. Read the following sentence several times, each time stressing a different one of the italicized words, and observe how significantly the meaning changes with each different reading:

I never *said* that *I dislike you.*

As long as we are mentioning the fallacy of accent, we ought to mention a few other types of distortions that are usually associated with it. The first is **quoting out of context.** For instance, an issue of *Time* magazine printed the following:

FLEECED AGAIN

The Federal Government sometimes uses its tax dollars to underwrite academic research that might charitably be described as frivolous. Among recipients of such largesse is Sociologist Pierre van den Berghe of the University of Washington, who used part of a $97,000 grant from the National Institute of Mental Health to underwrite a report by his researcher, George Primov, titled, "The Peruvian Brothel as Sexual Dispensary and Social Arena."

Primov made some 20 visits to the San Tutis brothel outside the Andean city of Cuzco. His interviews with the prostitutes led to the conclusion that brothels do serve as, among other things, a gathering place for drinking and storytelling.

Senator William Proxmire last week gave the study his Golden Fleece Award for "the biggest, most ridiculous or most ironic waste of taxpayers' money." Van den Berghe, the author of *Academic Gamesmanship,* professed to be pleased, saying: "My reputation in the academic community will be enhanced."

To which Mr. van den Berghe replied:

I am surprised that TIME should still opt for the same brand of cheap sensationalism as Senator Proxmire. Of the $97,000 of the NIMH grant in question, a maximum of $50 was spent on the brothel study. This minute aspect of the total project resulted in a single paragraph of 14 lines in a book of 324 pages where George Primov and I reported the results of our study, approximately the *one-thousandth* part of the total project. The book is entitled *Inequality in the Peruvian Andes; Class and Ethnicity in Cuzco.* That sounds sexy, doesn't it? If my study was about prostitution, then TIME is a pornographic magazine. It too occasionally mentions prostitution.

Pierre L. van den Berghe
University of Washington, Seattle

Now, if *Time* is guilty as charged, it has indeed been guilty of distorting the context of what actually occurred, and it has created an egregious straw man.

Quoting out of context can turn a person's words against him. Miss Thompson has just worked several hours overtime to type and Xerox a twenty-page report for her employer, Mr. Lannett. As she gives him the copies of the report, he looks at her and appreciatively exclaims, "Betty, you're terrific. I love you. Come, it's late, let me take you to dinner. Then I'll drive you home." An eavesdropper hears this exchange and reports that Mr. Lannett is in love with his secretary, tried to take her out to dinner, and wanted to take her home afterward.

A second variation of the fallacy of accent occurs by **quoting selectively**. For instance, an advertisement for a particular movie makes the following claim:

> Everyone is raving about the film. In fact, *Movie Magazine* described the film as *fantastic, unbelievable,* and *hypnotic.* The reviewer was at a loss for words to describe the impact that this movie had upon her.

Here is what the reviewer actually said:

> This movie is fantastic and unbelievable—it's hard to believe that such trash could come out of Hollywood. I am at a loss for words to describe the impact that the movie had upon me, but I'll try: tedious, boring, and hypnotic: it put me to sleep.

What is not said can be as damaging as what is said. You are asked, "Do you think Sally Santiss is honest?" You hesitate a bit, perhaps stammer, and then reply, "I'd better not answer that question. I really don't know her that well." You certainly have said nothing overtly to hurt Sally Santiss, but your indecision, hesitancy, and lack of positive support may indeed hurt her.

Here is another example. A teacher, writing a college recommendation for one of her students, responds to the following question: *Describe what you consider to be this student's most prominent strengths.* The teacher replies:

> Tom has been a student of mine now for three years. Throughout that time he has been conscientious. He has never cut class, and his work has always been handed in on time. He has been cheerful in class and has often participated in class discussions. He once was the rebuttalist in a class debate, where he spoke persuasively.

Now, the teacher has said nothing incriminating; she has said nothing to disparage the student; in fact, everything she has said is positive. There is not one overtly negative statement in the teacher's response. Yet, no college is likely to be impressed by such a response. What the teacher here has done is an example of what is known as **damnation by faint praise**, a variation of the fallacy of accent. The teacher has stressed only positive qualities, but those qualities are so weak and so insignificant that they actually appear as weaknesses.

Finally, no discussion of accent would be complete without the classic example. The anecdote appears in *The Old Shipmasters of Salem* by Charles E. Trow (G.P. Putnam's Sons, 1905):

> Captain L—— had a first mate who was at times addicted to the use of strong drink, and occasionally, as the slang saying has it, "got full." The ship was lying in a port in China, and the mate had been on shore and had there indulged rather freely in some of the vile compounds common in Chinese ports. He came on board, "drunk as a lord," and thought he had a mortgage on the whole world. The captain, who rarely ever touched liquors himself, was greatly disturbed by the disgraceful conduct of his officer, particularly as the crew had all observed his condition. One of the duties of the first officer is to write up the "log" each day, but as that worthy was not able to do it, the captain made the proper entry, but added: "The mate drunk all day." The ship left port the next day and the mate got "sobered off." He attended to his writing at the proper time, but was appalled when he saw what the captain had done. He went on deck, and soon after the following colloquy took place:
>
> "Cap'n, why did you write in the log yesterday that I was drunk all day?"
>
> "It was true, wasn't it?"
>
> "Well, 'lowing 't was, it was a bad thing to say about me."
>
> "It was true, wasn't it?"
>
> "Yes, but what will the owners say if they see it? 'T will hurt me with them."
>
> But the mate could get nothing more from the captain than, "It was true, wasn't it?"

The next day, when the captain was examining the book, he found at the bottom of the mate's entry of observation, course, winds, and tides: "The captain sober all day." He went on deck in high dudgeon, met the mate—who saw that a storm was brewing—and then another dialogue took place as follows:

"What did you mean, you rascal, by writing in the log that I was 'sober all day,' yesterday?"

"It was true, wasn't it, Cap'n?"

Amphiboly. The ambiguous position of a word in a sentence is called amphiboly. One cannot be sure just what the syntax of a word or group of words is. "The Philadelphia Singers are a popular music group." Are they a group that sings popular music? Or are they a music group that is popular? The word *popular* is amphibolous: Does it modify *music* or does it modify *music group?* Of course, in print the problem can be remedied with hyphens: *a popular-music group* as opposed to *a popular music-group*. But sometimes the amphiboly is more subtle. Take this newspaper classified ad that appears under *Furnished Apartments for Rent:*

3 rooms, river view, private phone, bath, kitchen, utilities included

Your interest is aroused. But when you visit the apartment, there is neither a bathroom nor a kitchen. You challenge the landlord. He remarks that there are common bathroom and kitchen facilities at the end of the hall. "But what about the private bath and kitchen that the ad mentioned?" you query. "What are you talking about?" the landlord replies. "The ad didn't say anything about a private bath or a private kitchen. All the ad said was *private phone.*" The advertisement was amphibolous. One cannot tell from the printed words whether *private* modifies only *phone* or whether it also modifies *bath* and *kitchen*.

Grammatical ambiguity. There are several sources of grammatical ambiguity. 1) Ambiguity can occur over whether a phrase is restrictive or non-restrictive.

This proposal is favored only by the workers who are eager to get something for nothing.

If the statement is written, there should be no problem, provided that the writer honors and the reader understands the principles of punctuation. But if the statement is spoken, it may be interpreted:

> This proposal is favored only by the workers, who
> are eager to get something for nothing.

The listener might interpret the statement to mean that all the workers are eager to get something for nothing. 2) Faulty or incomplete comparisons can contribute to ambiguity: "I like Leslie more than Louise." This statement can mean "I like Leslie more than I like Louise" or "I like Leslie more than Louise likes Leslie." An incomplete comparision, on the other hand, is so open-ended that we can't be sure what it means: "Shop at Super-Mart and pay less." *Less than what?* we should ask. 3) Then there are ambiguous references of pronouns:

> The police and the fire departments are threatening a strike,
> and the politicians are threatening reprisal. The newspapers
> claim that *their* statements are only causing further hostility.

Does the *their* refer to newspapers? To the policemen and firemen? To the politicians? (4) Specific words can be ambiguous:

> I won't help you because you're drunk.

Does this mean, "I will help you not because you're drunk but because of some other reason"? Or does it mean "The reason I won't help you is that you are drunk"?

> Prices have been reduced so you can shop with ease.

Does this mean "Prices have been reduced so that you can shop with ease"? or does it mean "Prices have been reduced; therefore, you can shop with ease"? We will meet more semantic problems in Chapter 20.

Juxtaposition. We have already seen in Chapter 6 how juxtaposition can suggest without stating. Two ostensibly unrelated statements or events appear in such a fashion that we are encouraged to infer a connection between them: "Did you hear that there was a shooting in the neighborhood last night? Oh, by the way, I understand that Raymond Spinner now keeps a gun in his house?" Is the speaker suggesting some connection between the shooting and Raymond Spinner? Or did the mention of a shooting merely remind the speaker that Spinner is now keeping a gun? Here is a more persuasive example: Two days after a newspaper reports on a scandal in City Hall, the mayor cancels a fund-raising dinner. We are tempted to infer that the mayor cancelled his fund-raising dinner because he is embarrassed by and perhaps even involved in the scandal and, realizing that things are hot, has decided that this a bad time for a fund-raising dinner. The facts, however, may be totally at odds with this inference. The mayor may have nothing to do with the alleged scandal; in fact, he may have known nothing about it. His cancelling the dinner may be for totally different reasons. He may realize that the local economy is in an unstable period, and these economic conditions may persuade him that this is not the time for fund-raising. He may even have decided to cancel the dinner before the newspaper reported the scandal.

Finally, there is the **enthymeme,** an argument which is incomplete. When I say "Tabby is a cat. I hate her," my utterance is incomplete. I have omitted a statement something like "I hate all cats." We constantly leave out premises in our utterances and expect people to make the necessary inferences. Usually there is no problem: The unstated premise is usually obvious. "Look at those clouds. I guess it's going to rain." The statement omitted here is most likely something like "Clouds such as these almost always bring rain" or "I heard on the latest weather forecast that we may get rain. Look at those clouds. I guess it is going to rain."

Needless to say, whenever a person has to make an inference, there is the danger of that inference being an incorrect one. Sometimes it may make no difference—as in the example just cited. The issue is not why you think it is going to rain; the issue is that it is going to rain. But sometimes an enthymematic expression can effect serious consequences. For instance, look back at the illustration cited in Chapter 8. The celebrity comments:

> Folks, you may not realize it, but I still get very nervous when I have to go on camera. Therefore, it's very important that I look my best. When those cameras come in for a

close-up, my teeth have to be as white as possible. There-fore, I use Pepomint. Pepomint makes my teeth white.

These statements seem to be a series of non sequiturs, and the celebrity making them appears to be a fool. But perhaps what appears to be stupid is merely an incomplete line of thought. Per-haps what the celebrity really means is something like this:

Folks, you may not realize it, but I still get very nervous when I have to go on camera; therefore, I need every bit of security that I can get. Pepomint contributes to my feeling of security. It makes my teeth white; therefore, at least I don't have to worry about my teeth when the camera comes in for a close-up.

Supplying the missing statements makes the celebrity's remarks seem much more sensible.

12

Confusion and Inference

*"But 'glory' doesn't mean a 'nice knock-down argu-
ment,'" Alice objected.*

*"When I use a word," Humpty Dumpty said, in
rather a scornful tone, "it means just what I choose it to
mean—neither more nor less."*

*"The question is," said Alice, "whether you can make
words mean so.many different things."*

*"The question is," said Humpty Dumpty, "which is to
be master—that's all."*

Lewis Carroll, *Through the Looking Glass*

Confusion can result from several sources: from inattention, from
imprecise phraseology, from hasty or incorrect inferences, from
misinterpretation, from ambiguity, from vagueness, from oversimplification, from the inability to distinguish the relevant from the
irrelevant, from the inability to distinguish an emotional appeal
from a logical one.

The misinterpretation of single words can lead to confusion.
Sometimes people make incorrect assumptions about the structure
and meaning of words. For instance, the word *inflammable*, they
will reason, means 'not easily set on fire,' because the prefix *in* often
negates a word: *inactive, inappropriate, inefficient*. They do not
realize that the prefix has another function: one of strengthening a
word, as in *institute, invaluable, include*. Hence, they will fail to
recognize that *flammable* and *inflammable* are synonymous.

Confusion can result when people use words without knowing
precisely what those words mean. For instance, a newspaper's account of a trial makes the following statement: "Judge Hart re-

mained disinterested throughout the proceedings of the trial." A person reading the account flares forth, "If the judge doesn't care, he shouldn't be a judge," and he proceeds to blast the judge's lack of concern. What has happened here is that the reader has confused *disinterested* with *uninterested,* and he has made a serious blunder.

There are many words in the language that have similar sounds but different meanings, for instance, *flout—flaunt; rational—rationalize; credible—creditable; delusion—allusion; prescribe—proscribe.* Many people do not realize that there is a distinction between each word in the pair; these people often use either word in the pair indiscriminately. When people confuse words such as these, what they think they are saying and what they actually say are two very different things.

Sometimes a person will know the general meaning of a word but not the subtleties or the connotations of that word. An article once mentioned a pianist who suddenly became so notorious that he was offered several recording contracts. Of course, *notorious* does mean *famous* but the two words are not synonyms. A notorious person is well-known for behavior of which we disapprove.

Another source of verbal confusion is the fact that, as words take on secondary meanings, their primary meanings sometimes become forgotten—the word *restive,* for instance. Some people will say that the word means "restful"; they simply are wrong. Other people will pride themselves on knowing the true meaning of the word: "restless." Well, the latter group is right, but only partially right. Rare is the person who realizes that the first meaning of the word is "unmanageable," "unruly," "stubborn," "uncooperative." Now, if three people hear the word *restive,* and each is sure that he knows what it means, and each assigns a different meaning to the word—(1) "restful" (2) "restless" (3) "unruly and uncooperative"— think of the confusion that can occur as the conversation continues.

Confusion can come from a word that has both a technical and a loose, often slang, usage. When I call someone a *bastard,* for instance, am I stating a fact, or am I expressing my dislike for that person? When I say that Belinda is guilty of manslaughter, someone who doesn't realize that the word *manslaughter* is technical rather than descriptive may conjure in his mind a highly lurid picture of Belinda, formulating her murderous plans and then slaughtering savagely her unfortunate victim. Many people use the word *sym-*

phony to describe classical music in general: a Chopin nocturne becomes a symphony. Others use the word *Victorian* as a synonym for conservative or prudish. I remember someone once describing Alexander Pope's poetry as Victorian—thereby completely ignoring the fact that Pope's poetry preceded Queen Victoria's reign by a full century. Then there's the language of psychiatry and psychology: *psychopath, schizophrenic, anal, psychotic, manic* . . . to name but just a few. Despite the fact that these words are each quite different and that each has a different medical denotation, they are frequently used interchangeably to describe any behavior that is odd or erratic. The vocabulary of medicine and psychology is a veritable grabbag for those who don't know what they're talking about. Beware of laymen spouting psychology!

Closely related to verbal confusion is the phenomenon that can occur when an **evaluative word** is used but **not defined.** For instance, suppose I refer to Miss Lasser as *crude.* Indeed, I have certain qualities in mind. That word, however, may mean something entirely different to you. Hence, unless I qualify my meaning, you will assign your meaning to the word and come up with an entirely different set of associations. Evaluative words mean different things to different people; hence, when several people hear an evaluative word, each person conjures up a different image, and each of those images may be far from what the speaker actually intended.

People sometimes simply abuse words. David Fischer in his book *Historians' Fallacies* makes a splendid observation:

> Historians have been known to write "always" for "sometimes," and "sometimes" for "occasionally," and "occasionally" for "rarely," and "rarely" for "once." In historical writing "certainly" sometimes means "probably," and "probably" means "possibly," and "possibly" means "conceivably."

Not only historians! I recall hearing a highly educated person remark: "I was amazed at the attendance of the meeting. Everyone was there. Only six people were missing." What does one say to a remark like that one. Does one shriek in outrage, insisting that if six people were absent, *everyone* wasn't present! Sometimes one gets the feeling that we are living in Alice's Wonderland where words mean whatever the utterer wants them to mean.

Fischer continues to describe the problem. Again, we should not limit his comments just to historians:

> Similarly the phrase "It needs no comment" should sometimes be translated "I do not know what comment it needs." When a historian writes, "It is unknown," he might mean "It is unknown to me," or "I don't know," or even "I won't tell." The expression "in fact" sometimes means merely "in my opinion," and the phrases "doubtless" or "undoubtedly" or "beyond the shadow of a doubt" sometimes really should be read, "An element of doubt exists which I, the author, shall disregard."

Equivocation is a frequent source of confusion. There are three common types of equivocation. The first occurs when a word has two or more different meanings and the different meanings are mixed together. Since the various meanings are not distinguished from each other, confusion enters. An advertisement for Disney World reads: "Isn't it time your fantasy world became a reality?" It is highly improbable that Disney World will cater to the fantasies of most adults. A more absurd example goes something like this: "James Monroe was a strong president. Therefore, when it comes time to preserve his house, we want a strong paint. Brand Z is being used. It's a strong paint befitting such a strong president. Therefore, use Brand Z."

Another type of equivocation occurs when the meaning of a word shifts during discourse. Let us look back at an example cited earlier in Chapter 8.

> We need penal reform and we need it immediately. Our prisons are places in which the God-given dignity of a man is plundered. In fact, the great humanitarian, Albert Schweitzer, said, "As long as one person is denied his essential rights and dignities as a human being, no one is free." Given the present conditions, ladies and gentlemen, neither you nor I am free.

There is equivocation on the word *free*. It is used first in its broadest sense: freedom of belief, worship, speech, and other freedoms granted by the Bill of Rights. Then it is used in a restrictive sense: the opposite of *imprisoned*, the physical sense of the word. This type of equivocation can be subtle and cause considerable confusion.

A third type of equivocation comes from relative words: "Eisenhower was a good general, a good citizen, a good father, a good golfer, a good American. Therefore, he will make a good president." The conclusion is a non sequitur. He might be the best general, the best citizen, the best father, the best golfer, the best American alive, but these qualities do not mean that he will be a good president. Here is another example: "The Chrysler Building is a building; it is also a small skyscraper; therefore, the Chrysler Building is a small building." Not true, of course. An adjective cannot be shifted from one noun to another without changing or distorting the meaning.

Fustianism (also see *gobbledygook* and *jargonese* in Chapter 6) can contribute to confusion. Bombastic, pretentious, fancy, inflated language and ideas can sometimes camouflage the fact that a speaker has nothing of consequence to say, is speaking nonsense, that he doesn't know what he is talking about, that he is just throwing words around, and that his words mean nothing: "If we are to talk about *void*, then we must define it and, if we can define it, then it must exist, and if it exists, then it is a thing, for nothing that exists cannot not be a thing—whether that thing be palpable or abstract. Definition predicates cognizance of intrinsic quiddity, and if one can ascertain quiddity, then one must also acknowledge ontology, and the acceptance of ontology invariably establishes satisfaction of the *onus probandi*."

People hearing such claptrap may be impressed and they may confuse pretentiousness with erudition.

Double standards can contribute to confusion. A double standard can occur when a person claims to sponsor a certain belief except when that belief applies to him. The old epigram "Do what I say, not what I do" is often implicit. People frequently alter their standards and beliefs to suit their own convenience. Mr. Hendricks, a struggling businessman, vociferously believes that the rich should be heavily taxed ... until he himself becomes rich; he then promptly changes his tune. Mrs. Galvin inveighs against the dope-smoking youth culture . . . until her son is caught smoking: "Well, you know, it's really not that serious," she remarks to her neighbor; "all kids try it; at least he's not drinking." George Orwell described this phenomenon as **doublethink:** the ability to entertain simultaneously two contradictory beliefs.

Sometimes a person seems to be guilty of doublethink when he merely has not articulated his true motivation. A group of executives are trying to decide on a time for a meeting; it is Monday morning:

MR. B.: Well, we're all tied up Tuesday morning and afternoon. Why don't we meet Tuesday night after supper?

MR. D.: No, no, please! Anytime but evenings. Evening meetings are terrible. I find myself worn out by evening, and I've noticed that evening meetings are never very productive. Besides, we won't have enough time.

MR. G.: Well, what about Wednesday, either morning or afternoon?

MR. B.: I'm afraid that I'll be out of town all day Wednesday.

MR. H.: Well, we've got to meet before Thursday. That leaves this afternoon. How about four P.M. today?

MR. D.: No, that's not very good. We won't have enough time . . . we'll feel rushed. How about tonight, say nine P.M. We can stay in town and have a leisurely supper and be refreshed for a nine o'clock meeting—it won't take very long, anyway.

At this point, the executives may be ready to strangle Mr. D. He just said that he doesn't like evening meetings, and now he's suggesting an evening meeting . . . and one, furthermore, that won't begin until nine P.M. He just vetoed the four P.M. meeting because "we won't have enough time," and now he says that the meeting "won't take very long, anyway." How does one explain such a contradiction?

What has happened is this: Mr. D. is very eager to see the final game of the World Series on television, scheduled to begin in the late afternoon. At the same time, he is a bit embarrassed to say that a baseball game is the reason for his inconveniencing everyone else. Therefore, he acts out of expediency. He impulsively latches on to the only other available time, Monday night, and he selects a time to suit his convenience, nine P.M., an hour that will give him plenty of time to get home and watch his game before the meeting. True, he doesn't like evening meetings, but he is willing to endure any inconvenience as long as he can watch the game. His colleagues may regard him as a fool because they are unaware of his true motivation, but Mr. D. is willing to forego both credibility and consistency for his personal reasons.

The problem of standards is often significant. All of us do not always approach a situation from the same perspectives and standards. Confusion results when these different points of departure are not identified. We may then talk at cross purposes. For instance, Ellen, a secretary for Mr. Holt, suffers from migraine headaches and consequently she is frequently absent from the office. A migraine attack sometimes forces her to miss two or three days in a row. Now, one day Mr. Ballard, head of the company, inquires about Ellen. In the course of the conversation, Mr. Ballard asks, "Does she take her job seriously?" Mr. Holt answers, "Well, I don't see how she can take her job very seriously. I can't blame her for missing time because of her migraine. But the work on her desk piles up and she gets far behind. Even when her desk is loaded, she still goes home every day at five P.M.—she never bothers to stay overtime—she doesn't cut short her lunch hour to try to get caught up, she doesn't come on Saturdays to try to get caught up. In fact, right now we're several days behind in our paperwork. No, I don't think she does take her job all that seriously."

The problem here is that Mr. Holt is evaluating the situation only from his perspective. It is very possible that Ellen does take her job very seriously, that Mr. Holt has never specifically asked her to put in extra time in order to get caught up, and that it has never occurred to Ellen to come to the office on her own time. It is also possible that the personnel director told Ellen that her hours were 9 A.M. to 5 P.M. unless she were specifically told otherwise. Therefore, from her point of view, she is doing her job to the best of her ability, and Mr. Holt's statement is an unfair one.

Another type of confusion comes from **circular reasoning**, sometimes referred to as **begging the question.** When an argument uses one of its premises as a conclusion, that argument is said to be circular. It proves nothing; it merely restates one of its premises under the guise of proving that premise. The following two illustrations will clarify the principle of circular reasoning:

Samuelson's books on economics are used in schools and colleges throughout the nation because Samuelson is an authority on economics. No one could deny that he is an authority, and a significant one at that. We know that he is an authority because his books are used in schools and colleges throughout the country. If he weren't an authority, his books wouldn't be so widely used.

If you wear expensive suits, then you may make a favorable impression on employers. Then, if you make a favorable impression, you may get the job. If you get the job, then you will have an excellent salary, and if you have a good salary, you'll be able to afford expensive clothing.

The formula goes something like this:

Since statement A is true, statement B is true.
Since statement B is true, statement A is true.
Therefore, statement A is true.

But we knew all along that statement A was true; therefore nothing has been proved.

Circular reasoning is sometimes used for humorous effect:

MARTHA: George, do you remember all those times when we were dating and my father would be waiting up for us? Well, I actually wanted him to be there.
GEORGE: Why?
MARTHA: I didn't want to be alone with you in such comfortable circumstances.
GEORGE (apprehensively): Why?
MARTHA: Because I was afraid of what I would do. I was

afraid that I might not be able to control myself.

GEORGE: Oh, there was nothing to worry about. I wouldn't have done anything.

MARTHA: (apprehensively): Why?

GEORGE: Because your father was there.

INFERENCES

A host of confusions come from faulty inferences. People misinterpret words or statements, assume more than they have a right to assume, inappropriately read between the lines, infer a cause and effect relationship when there is not one, and generalize from insufficient data.

Sometimes the complement of a word is confused with the opposite of that word. For instance, the complement of *good* is *not good;* the opposite is *bad.* The two are quite different. If I say that a performance was not good, I am not saying that it was a bad one. Similarly, if I say "Mr. Bingham doesn't like you," I am not saying that Mr. Bingham dislikes you. In the same way, if two people are expressing a different point of view and I agree with one of the persons, I am not necessarily disagreeing with the other person or implying that the other person is wrong; yet that other person may assume that I am disagreeing.

A term can have three degrees: the presence of the quality that the term denotes, the absence of that quality, and the presence of the opposite of that quality. The intermediate degree, the complement, merely states that the quality is absent; it says no more; it is neutral and noncommittal.

Term	*Complement*		*Opposite*
good	not good	not bad	bad
like	do not like	do not dislike	dislike

If one is to treat the language with respect, one must not cross the vertical lines that separate the term from its complement and the complement from the opposite. In fact, negatives can cause such problems that it would be a good idea to avoid them wherever possible and to phrase statements in the affirmative. Therefore, instead of saying "The performance wasn't good," it would be better to be more precise: "The performance was fair" or "The performance was neither bad nor good, merely satisfactory" or "The performance was mediocre" or "The performance was nondescript." And instead of saying "Mr. Bingham doesn't like you," it would be better to say, "Mr. Bingham neither likes nor dislikes you" or "Mr. Bingham doesn't have strong feelings about you one way or the other." If it is impractical to phrase the statement in the affirmative, then at least make it clear that you do not intend to imply the opposite.

Then there is the fallacy of **composition.** This fallacy occurs when one projects the properties of the parts to the property of the whole: "If it's true for each of the parts, then it's true for the whole." Such an inference, however, is not necessarily true. Take an orchestra, for instance. Just because every member of an orchestra is a superb performer does not necessarily mean that the orchestra as a whole performs superbly; the members may not be able to work together. The fallacy of composition ignores the relationships among the parts. What is true for each of the parts is not necessarily true for the whole.

The fallacy of composition can lead to hasty generalizations and to stereotyping. This occurs when the behavior of an individual or of certain individuals of a group is projected upon all the members of that group. Because a handful of students from College X cause a fracas at a local bar, some people will regard all the students of College X as troublemakers.

The reverse process gives us the fallacy of **division,** the assumption that what is true for the whole is also true for each of the parts. Someone will argue that, because an orchestra plays superbly, each member of that orchestra is a superb soloist. Someone will assume that because Stephen got into Yale, he must have been a superb high school student. Now, it is true that Yale takes many superb high school students, but it also takes some students because their parents are wealthy or because the father is an alumnus or because the applicant has some unique talent. Therefore, it is not completely safe to infer that Stephen was a superb high school student.

Another fallacy is the fallacy of **improper distribution** or the fallacy of **addition.** This fallacy assumes that you can add items that cannot be added. A school administrator argues, "Let's cut out the pledge of allegiance each morning. We'll be able to save two minutes a day. That's ten minutes a week. That'll be the equivalent of an entire extra day by the end of the year." Such computation is true on paper only. The extra two minutes a day is, in fact, negligible. The school board of a major city used this fallacy to regain time lost from a recent blizzard. Faced with the problem of how to make up the time during which the schools were closed because of the blizzard, they simply extended the school day by a half hour.

Someone once mused: "If they would just put zippers on pajamas instead of buttons, I could save twenty seconds a day, that's over two minutes a week, a couple hours a year, and three or four days in a lifetime." The fallacy is that you cannot collect and store the seconds you would save each time you zip your pajamas instead of buttoning them.

A variation of this fallacy occurs when people try to redistribute something, claiming that "as long it all comes out the same in the end, everything will be fine." An administrator says to a football coach, "You will not be able to have ninety minutes a day, Monday through Thursday, for football practice. However, don't worry: You won't lose anything. You can have from noon until six P.M. on Fridays."

The problem here is that a football team needs time each day; its improvement is gradual and cumulative. The administrator has fallaciously presumed that six hours is six hours, no matter how it is distributed, that a team can get the same results from one six-hour session as from four ninety-minute sessions. The administrator has ignored the law of diminishing returns: the fact that after a while the long practice will become unproductive.

A similar fallacy occurs when an agency tells a constituent that it will be unable to supply funds for a few months but that it will compensate by supplying double the funds later. The Welfare Department, for instance, says that it will not be able to issue any checks for April but that it will double the amount of the checks for May. What the department is forgetting is that people cannot stop eating in April and then compensate by eating double the amount in May.

Definition because of common characteristics. You assume that a person or a thing is a member of a particular group just because that person or thing shares a quality with other members of that

group. "All Communists distrust capitalism. Harriet distrusts capitalism. Therefore, Harriet is a Communist." The conclusion is not
necessarily true. Just because Harriet distrusts capitalism does not
automatically make her a Communist. People other than Communists also distrust capitalism. The technical name for fallacies of
this type is the fallacy of the **undistributed middle.** We will see
further examples of this later.

Opinion, inference, speculation, and attitude are often confused
with fact. This misunderstanding often manifests itself as rumor.
David tells Philip that he is dissatisfied with his job; Philip tells
Linda that David is thinking of quitting his job; Linda tells Sam
that David is quitting; and so the story goes. People often think
aloud, and when they do so, they occasionally express sentiments to
which they may not be wholly committed. To repeat such sentiments is irresponsible.

A TV program did a feature on the type of life that Americans
were experiencing in Argentina. At the end of the feature, an inter-
viewee was asked something like this: "If the Americans here had
the viable choice of staying here or leaving, which do you think
they'd choose?" The person thought for a moment and replied, "I
think they'd go." Now, suppose Mr. and Mrs. Brown were watching
this interview. Mr. Brown's company has asked him to move to
Argentina; Mrs. Brown, however, is totally against the move. It
would be natural for her to say, "See, George, what have I been
telling you! We won't like it there. Don't take my word for it—
we've just had proof. The Americans there now want to get out."
Mrs. Brown has heard what she wanted to hear. She heard the
opinion of one person and is treating that opinion as fact. The
person being interviewed may be right or he may be wrong, but
there was no reason to equate one man's opinion with fact.

A very dangerous type of fallacy occurs when people confuse
all with *some* or *one* with *most.* Many people assume that, because
some citizens feel a certain way, this is the way all or most citizens
feel. Even worse, many people project a single opinion upon the
group as a whole: Because one person feels a certain way, everyone
feels that way. The illustration cited in the previous prargraph is an
example. Mrs. Brown regards the opinion of one man as representative of the whole group of Americans living in Argentina. This is a
variation of the fallacy of composition, but, whereas the fallacy of

composition assumes that what is true for the parts is true also for the whole, the *all/some* or *one/most* fallacy assumes that what is true for some of the parts is also true for all of the parts or that what is true for one of the parts is also true for most or all of the parts.

This process can apply to isolated incidents. A lesbian gets caught stealing. "I always knew you couldn't trust them lesbians," remarks the dolt, projecting the behavior of one person upon the whole class and merely using the incident to support his prejudice. Someone gets into an accident because the crack in his windshield burst; some politician immediately sponsors legislation to make it illegal to drive with any crack whatsoever in one's windshield. Two or three members of the city government are discovered to have embezzled: "The whole goverment is a bunch of crooks," remarks someone.

All these illustrations are examples of overreacting, of making a hasty generalization, of oversimplifying, of assuming that what is true of a part is also true of the other parts. The *all/some* fallacy is insidious, yet it is remarkably common. It leads to stereotyping, to bigotry and prejudice, and to terribly wrong conclusions.

Cause and Effect

*"Why are you standing here on this street corner,
     wildly waving your hands and shouting?"*
"I'm keeping away the elephants."
"But there aren't any elephants here."
"You bet: that's why I'm here."

Traditional Tale

The study of cause and effect relationships can be a complex one. For purposes of this chapter, we will deal with some of the common types of confusion that stem from faulty cause and effect inferences.

First, we should identify three types of causes, or conditions. **Necessary cause** or **condition:** If Y cannot happen unless X is present, X is a necessary cause or condition for Y. Knowing the keyboard of a piano is a necessary condition for playing the piano: You cannot play the piano unless you know the keyboard. Getting oxygen is a necessary condition for living: a person cannot live without oxygen.

Sufficient cause or **condition:** If Y always occurs when X is present, then X is a sufficient condition (or cause) of Y. Grabbing a hot piece of iron is a sufficient condition for getting burned. It is not a necessary cause since one can get burned in countless other ways. Hence:

Grabbing a hot piece of iron
Touching a hot stove
Spilling boiling water ————————► getting burned
Touching a hot coal
Letting a lighted match burn too low

Any of those five conditions—and countless other conditions—is sufficient to cause a person to get burned.

Contributory cause or **condition:** If X is one of several factors that can cause Y, then X is a contributory cause or condition of Y. Smoking heavily is a contributory cause of lung cancer. It is not a necessary cause, since people can get lung cancer from other sources. And it is not a sufficient cause, since not all heavy smokers get lung cancer.

We can now summarize these three types of causal relationships:

> If X does not happen, then Y will not happen: *necessary* cause or condition.
> If X happens, Y will happen: *sufficient* cause or condition.
> If X happens, Y may happen: *contributory* cause or condition.

A common type of fallacy occurs when people do not distinguish among these three relationships, when, for instance, a contributory cause is confused with a sufficient cause. People confuse *a* reason with *the* reason. The statement "Smoking causes lung cancer" is an example. The statement should be rephrased: "Smoking may cause lung cancer" or "Smoking is a leading cause of lung cancer." Such confusion is a type of oversimplification and is often a hasty generalization.

Sometimes the oversimplification is camouflaged in verbiage:

> Are you frustrated with your job? Do you feel held back, dissatisfied? Do you feel that your potential is being untapped? Do you look at your boss and say, 'I'm better than he is. I could do a better job!'
> It's true that many able people do not rise to the top. Now, statistics show that image is important—how you project and carry yourself. If you want to get ahead, you've got to be aggressive and confident. You can't sit back and wait for opportunity to come to you.
> That's why *Personal Dynamics* was founded: to help people like you. *Personal Dynamics* is a group of professionals who have studied the components of leadership and who are trained to help you. They will show you how to put

your best foot forward, how to make others realize that you are as good as you know you are.

Therefore, if you want to get ahead, come to *Personal Dynamics*. We will make a new person out of you.

Stripped of its verbiage, this pitch confuses contributory cause with both necessary and sufficient cause. It implies that you will not get ahead unless you change your image (necessary cause) and that if you change your image you will get ahead (sufficient cause). What it should say is that *Personal Dynamics may* help you to change your image and that, if you change your image, you *may* be in a better position to get ahead.

A second type of abuse of cause and effect relationships occurs when people confuse necessary and sufficient conditions:

SPOKESMAN GREEN: We cannot improve the plight of the people in the ghettos unless we make a concerted effort to find jobs for the thousands of people who are unemployed.

SPOKESMAN GRAY: That's nonsense! What about the thousands of youths who roam the streets, robbing innocent people so that they can get money to support their drug habits?

Green is citing a necessary condition: The ghettos cannot be improved unless people are employed. Gray, on the other hand, is citing a sufficient condition: Getting people jobs isn't sufficient to improve the ghettos. The problem here is that Green never said that providing jobs was the only answer; he merely said that it was a necessary step. The two spokesmen are not necessarily disagreeing; they are merely arguing at cross purposes.

Another type of confusion occurs when **remote cause** is not distinguished from **immediate cause**. Take the old chestnut:

> For want of a nail, the shoe was lost.
> For want of a shoe, the horse was lost.
> For want of a horse, the rider was lost.
> For want of a rider, the message was lost.
> For want of a message, the legion was lost.

For want of a legion, the battle was lost.
For want of a battle, the country was lost.

Therefore, one can reason that the country was lost because someone did not have a nail.

How far back can one go in assigning cause? There is no answer
to this question, but surely one has to use one's sense. And one has
to be wary of the tendency to rationalize. For example: Mr. Anderson, having too many whiskeys under his belt, gets into an auto-
mobile accident and wrecks the car. When he returns home, he
laces into his wife:

It's all your fault. If it hadn't been for you, this never would
have happened. If you hadn't spent everything in our check-
ing account, I wouldn't have been so upset. If I hadn't been
so upset, we wouldn't have fought. If we hadn't fought, I
wouldn't have gotten so mad that I had to get out of the
house. If I hadn't been so mad, I wouldn't have gone to
Kelsey's and had those whiskeys. If I hadn't had those whiskeys, I wouldn't have gotten into the accident. It's all your
fault.

Now, by no stretch of the imagination can Mr. Anderson blame
his wife for the accident. The immediate cause of the accident was
his drunkenness. If Anderson feels that he has to get drunk, that's
his business, but he knows that he shouldn't drive when he is drunk.
If he's going to drive when drunk, then he's going to have to assume
responsibility for the wreck. His reasoning is sheer rationalization.

Take the cause and effect relationship implied by the following
statement: "I fumbled because I stayed up too late last night study-
ing for my midterm exam in economics." We can respond to this
statement in at least four ways: (1) The speaker is confusing contributory with sufficient cause, i.e., he is assigning *a* cause as *the*
cause. (2) He is rationalizing. (3) He is assigning a minor cause as
the major cause. (4) He is assigning a remote cause as an immediate
cause. And he is probably implying a fifth relationship, a necessary
cause: "If I hadn't stayed up late, I wouldn't have fumbled."

Another fallacy occurs when cause and effect are reversed:

> We should definitely require all students to take art courses.
> The most creative students in the school are art majors. We
> certainly want our graduates to be creative. Therefore, the
> more art courses they take, the more creative they will be-
> come.

Does the art department make students creative? Or do the most
creative students in the school gravitate toward the art department?

> Biting one's fingernails makes a person nervous and edgy. I
> know a dozen people who bite their fingernails and they're
> all highstrung. If you want to be a more relaxed person, stop
> biting your fingernails.

The speaker here has got the cause and effect relationship back-
ward. It is not that biting one's fingernails makes a person nervous.
Rather, the fact is that nervous people tend to bite their fingernails.

> Of course Mrs. Burton feels that French is the most beauti-
> ful language in the world. After all, she did major in French
> and she travels to France whenever possible. Naturally she
> has to say that French is great.

It is much more likely that Mrs. Burton majored in French because
she felt that it was such a beautiful language and not, as the speaker
fallaciously suggests, that she defends her attitude toward French
because she majored in it.

Cause and effect relationships can be abused when a temporal
phenomenon is confused with a causal one. For instance, there is
the *post hoc* fallacy. The name comes from the Latin phrase *post
hoc, ergo propter hoc:* "after this, therefore because of this." This
fallacy occurs when a person argues that because event Y happened
after event X, it happened because of event X. The classic example
is the tribesman who beats his tom-tom each morning and assumes
that, since darkness fades after he beats his drum, the darkness
fades because he has beaten his drum. Most superstitions fall into
this category: "The reason I slipped on the ice was that I walked

under the ladder this morning." This fallacy accounted for some of
the criticism levied against the Carter administration for recognizing mainland China. It was argued that the reason that China attacked Vietnam in early 1979 was that the United States had
recognized China. Now, there may be *some* truth to this speculation—we may never know the whole truth. The point is, however,
that it is fallacious to reason that China attacked Vietnam *because*
of the recent support given by the Carter administration, merely
since the attack occurred after the administration gave its support.

> Since Mayor Garrison took office three months ago, there
> have been no instances of corruption in city government.
> The city is clearly indebted to the mayor for reinstating
> honesty in city government.

There is much that could be challenged in the above argument. But
for now we can merely say that unless there is solid evidence to
indicate that Mayor Garrison is solely responsible for the absence
of corruption, the argument is not a solid one. Isn't it possible that
there are several factors that have contributed to the absence of
corruption?

A variation of the *post hoc* fallacy occurs when a person argues
that because two events occur simultaneously, there is a cause and
effect relationship between them.

> Ever since we have entered our age of technology, espe-
> cially with our emphasis upon computers, we have noticed a
> move away from religion. The attendance at church services
> is markedly less than it was before computers entered the
> scene, and many denominations have decried their falling
> membership. Clearly, people have felt such a sense of mas-
> tery and confidence because of the computer that they have
> less of a need for religion. Technology has become the new
> god.

It is fallacious to say that, because the rise of technology and the
fall of religious support have occurred at the same time, one caused
the other. There are too many other factors that this argument

overlooks: the fact that many religious denominations have not changed with the times; the fact that people are less receptive to authority than they once were; the fact that many people have found an irresolvable conflict between their personal beliefs and religious teachings.

Another variation occurs when a person jumps to conclusions. This fallacy is sometimes referred to as *non causa pro causa:* "not a cause [mistaken] for a cause." Mr. Caron is robbed and assumes that the robbery was a personal affront. More likely than not, the robber merely found Mr. Caron's place an easy hit and took advantage of the opportunity; nothing personal was intended.

"So many of the stars in Hollywood are blondes. If I want to be a star, I'd better dye my hair blond." Again, here is the fallacy of the false cause. Stars do not become stars *because* they are blondes. It may help to be blond, but the speaker has confused a coincidence with a cause and effect relationship.

Then there is the fallacy of the false conclusion, a fallacy that we have already seen in the chapter on irrelevance. In this fallacy a group of reasons support a conclusion that is improper, irrelevant, and inappropriate:

> Boss: You have been late to work every day now for a week. That's enough reason for me to fire you and to hire my brother-in-law, who has wanted to work here for some time now.

Two points may be made: (1) There may not be sufficient reason to fire the clerk. It is possible that the clerk has never been warned; it is possible that there have been good reasons for the clerk's being late; and it is possible that the boss never inquired into those reasons. Rather than fire the clerk, the logical conclusion to the boss' problem may be to warn the clerk. (2) But even if the clerk is totally irresponsible, there is not necessarily any good reason for the boss to hire his brother-in-law, unless nepotism is considered a good reason.

> The present welfare program has been a botch ever since it began. All sorts of people are getting welfare who aren't

entitled to it, and the government seems to be making no
effort to screen those who are ineligible. Therefore, let's get
rid of this whole welfare system.

The fact that there are inequities and abuses in the present welfare
program does not lead to the conclusion that the welfare program
should be scrapped. The logical conclusion is that the government
take measures to tighten up the system and to remove those inequities. Cancelling the whole welfare program is like the proverbial throwing out of the baby with the bath water.

Finally, red herrings can enter a cause and effect relationship,
just as they can enter into any type of discussion:

You say that stock car racing is dangerous. But I think it's
unfair and shortsighted of you to criticize it. A lot of people
enjoy watching the races, and through these races a lot of
people are able to release potentially aggressive instincts,
energies that might otherwise become hostile and antisocial.

What the speaker says is true but irrelevant. The issue is the fact
that sports car racing is dangerous. Through a clever ploy, the
speaker has gone after a red herring and has made stock car racing
acceptable according to a criterion that was never the issue.

Establishing a legitimate or true cause from an apparent cause
is often a tricky matter. Sometimes it is indeed difficult to determine what is a true cause and what is merely an accompanying
circumstance. One of the chief problems is a lack of objectivity.
Many people assign a cause and effect relationship to confirm their
prejudices or to rationalize their errors or inadequacies. They jump
to conclusions because they do not take the time and energy to get
all the facts, to investigate carefully, to analyze, and to be
objective.

Interlude: Cause and Effect

Nothing is ever so simple as it first seems.
Murphy's Third Law

The conclusion of the previous chapter suggested that it is easy to improperly assign a cause and effect relationship and that people, unwilling to think rigorously and analytically, often oversimplify and jump to erroneous conclusions. This chapter offers some suggestions on how to avoid jumping to hasty conclusions.

In this discussion, event X will be the effect or the result, and event Y will be the alleged reason for that result or effect.

First, determine whether event X always occurs when event Y is present. If X always occurs when Y is present, Y is probably at least a contributory cause of X.

Second, determine whether event X ever occurs when event Y is absent. If X never occurs when Y is absent, the evidence is even stronger that Y is at least a contributory cause of X.

Third, examine event Y, the event that you think is the cause. Break that event down into every possible component: Y_1, Y_2, Y_3, and so on.

Fourth, determine whether event X is ever absent when one of those components is absent. If it is, then it is likely that not event Y but some aspect of event Y is the cause.

Fifth, determine whether event X ever occurs when only one of those components of Y is present. If it does, then the evidence is even stronger that the component of Y and not Y itself is the cause.

Let us put these steps into practice. Situation: I notice that whenever I drink three or more cups of coffee, I get a headache that lasts for about an hour; therefore, I conclude that drinking three or more cups of coffee gives me headaches.

Event X = the headache; event Y = drinking three or more cups of coffee.

Step 1: This is easy. I already know that three cups of coffee gives me a headache. But I still experiment. On one day, I have those three cups between 8 A.M. and 9 A.M. On another day I stretch out the cups: I have those three cups between 8 A.M. and 10 A.M. On another day, I have no coffee in the morning but rather I have my three cups between 2 P.M. and 4 P.M. On another day I have no coffee until after supper: I drink my three cups between 8 P.M. and 10 P.M. On still another day, I have my coffee before breakfast and none after breakfast. There are other variations that I may use in this part of the experiment. If I continue to have headaches after the third cup of coffee in each of these variations, then I am pretty sure that there is something associated with the coffee that is giving me headaches, i.e., the coffee is contributing to my headaches. At this point, I cannot say anything more definite.

But if in any one of those variations I do not get a headache, then I know that it is not the coffee but the coffee in combination with some other factor. For instance, I might get the headaches only when I drink three cups after breakfast, or only when I drink them without having had breakfast, or only when I drink them in the morning, or only when I drink them in too close succession.

If I continue to get headaches in each of the variations that I tried in Step 1, then I will move on to Step 2. I will see what happens when I have only two cups of coffee. I try the same variations that I tried in Step 1. If I do not get headaches after each of these variations, then I am even more sure that three or more cups of coffee is a contributory reason for my headaches.

At this point, do I have to stop having three or more cups of coffee a day? Perhaps, but not necessarily so. While I strongly suspect that three or more cups is a contributory cause, I have not established that it is either a sufficient or a necessary cause.

Therefore, I move to Step 3. This step is a nuisance. I take the act of having three or more cups of coffee and I break it down into as many components as I can:

—Is it any coffee, or a particular brand of coffee?

—Is it any type of coffee, or just regular coffee, or decaffeinated?

—Is the proportion of water to coffee always the same?

—Do I tend to smoke when I drink coffee?

—Does the presence or absence of sugar, or milk, or both have any effect?

—Is there any other event that always either precedes, accompanies, or follows my drinking of the coffee?

What I am trying to do here is to determine whether there is any single factor that in and of itself, or in combination with coffee, causes me to have headaches. For instance, it may be the combination of sugar and coffee that gives me headaches. It may be that I substitute saccharin for sugar; the only time that I have saccharin is when I have coffee; perhaps it is the saccharin and not the coffee that makes me ill. Or perhaps, without my realizing it, I always smoke when I drink coffee; perhaps it is the combination of coffee and cigarettes that gives me headaches. Maybe it's a particular brand of coffee. Perhaps I'm making my coffee too strong.

The point here is that I may be able to drink as much coffee as I want if I make one minor change, e.g., if I stop smoking every time I have coffee, or if I discontinue the saccharin, or if I don't make it as strong.

Having been successful with Step 4, I do not need to pursue Step 5. If, however, I have exhausted the possibilities of exploring the component parts of coffee and I am still getting my headaches, then I can be pretty sure that my original hypothesis was correct. I can't be positive, however, because I can never completely exhaust the possibilities. There may be all sorts of thing I haven't thought of. There may be some impurity in the water that reacts with the coffee to give me headaches; there may be a medical reason that I am unaware of.

One of the problems with cause and effect is that we often confuse the apparent cause with the true cause. In the illustration just cited, the apparent cause was coffee. The real cause was perhaps the saccharin or the combination of coffee and cigarettes. Another problem is that we often do not recognize that what appears to be one cause is often a combination of causes: the coffee *and* cigarettes; having the three cups of coffee *before* breakfast.

Sometimes people assign a cause and effect relationship that cannot be either proven or disproven. Take this example:

> In 1969, a Youth League was formed in Meriville. Its founder and director was Mr. Paul Lancer. The Youth League met in the basement of St. Jude's Church. It is a known fact that in 1970 and 1971 there was considerable damage done to St. Jude's basement. Neighbors of St. Jude's will also unanimously attest to the fact that the youngsters in these days were rowdy, often uncouth, and troublesome. Because of the rowdiness, the neighbors could always tell when the Youth League was meeting.
>
> Mr. Lancer left the program in 1972. Mr. Kenneth Marsh took over and is still running the program. Neighbors nowadays notice that the Youth League is much less rowdy. Many times they do not even realize that the League is meeting. The officials of St. Jude's have not noticed any damage in over two years.

Can we say that the reason for the improvement is Mr. Marsh's leadership?

Immediately, we note that we cannot apply the steps that the earlier part of this chapter suggested. Several years have elapsed since Mr. Lancer ran the Youth League—we cannot put his administration to the test.

But we should have enough sense to insist upon the following question: Are there any other factors that might have contributed to this improvement? We may phrase the question more professionally: Is the *only* difference between the present attractive conditions and the earlier unattractive conditions the difference in leadership? And, just for purposes of helping to clarify the issues, we might ask people who have been with the Youth League from its inception to speculate on what might have occurred had the Marsh and Lancer administrations been reversed.

Immediately we note an important factor: Lancer started the program. He had nothing to fall back upon; the program had no roots in Meriville. A new program does not have a collective sense of identity and purpose; such a sense has to develop gradually. Then we can observe that Lancer began the program in the late 1960s. Immediately we must recall that the youth in general throughout the country at that time was volatile, far less stable than in later years; the late 60s and early 70s were turbulent years for much of the youthful population. Finally, we should note that the Youth League was new not only to itself but also to the neighbors of St. Jude's.

Therefore, we note that the difference in administrators is not the only significant difference in the program. The times have changed significantly; the youth culture is not as refractory and unstable as it was ten years earlier; the neighbors have become used to youngsters, whereas it is possible that for quite a while after the program had been started, youngsters were seen as a threat. The program, now over a decade old, is more established; its goals are more clearly defined; and the members have more of a collective sense of identity. All of these factors are significant ones, and it is quite possible that the combination of them is responsible for the improved image of the Youth League.

Can we say that the reason for the improvement is Mr. Marsh's leadership? No. We can say, however, that his leadership has been a contributing factor. And if we learn from some disinterested third parties who were on the scene during both the Lancer and the Marsh administrations that in fact Lancer was not interested in maintaining order, that he was too permissive, that he did not keep a close watch on the youngsters and that in fact Marsh is very interested in maintaining order and considers the image of the organization as a high priority and keeps a close eye upon the youngsters under his charge, then we can say that Marsh is a significant factor. But we cannot say he is *the* reason.

Oversimplification

*"My friends," says he, "what is this which we now be-
hold as being spread before us? Refreshment. Do we need
refreshment, my friends? Because we are but mortal, because we are but sinful, because we are but of the earth,
because we are not of the air. Can we fly, my friends? We
cannot. Why can we not fly, my friends?"*

*Mr. Snagsby, presuming on the success of his last
point, ventures to observe in a cheerful and rather knowing tone, "No wings."*

Dickens, *Bleak House*, XIX

The tendency to oversimplify is common; probably all of us have
yielded to it at one time or another. We oversimplify when we seek
a quick, easy solution to a complex problem, when we don't want
to be bothered with the ramifications of an issue, and when we
respond glibly and hastily. Several of the items mentioned in the
chapters on propaganda, on emotionalism, and on confusion were
examples of oversimplification. The following discussion identifies
some additional types.

Accident. The fallacy of accident is committed when a general
rule is applied to a situation in which it was not intended to apply.
This fallacy suggests that there are no exceptions to a general rule
or principle. It acknowledges the letter of the law but ignores the
spirit of that law. For instance, it is night; the fog is heavy, and the
roads are wet. Mrs. Borden tells her husband to drive more slowly.
"What do you mean," he replies. "The speed limit is fifty-five: I'm
not going over the speed limit." Mr. Borden here is using the fallacy of accident. He is ignoring the fact that the particular road

conditions make the 55 mph speed limit inapplicable. Those who cite the commandment *Thou shalt not kill* to condemn warfare or capital punishment or euthanasia or abortion are judged by their opponents to commit this fallacy.

The **complex question.** A complex question occurs when an issue is posed that has several ramifications but whose ramifications are either ignored or not recognized: "Should we accept the proposal, yes or no?" There may be some parts of the proposal that are desirable but others that are undesirable. The complex question often includes two or more separate questions under the guise of one question: "Are you still cheating?" This question actually entails two separate questions: "Are you cheating now? Have you ever cheated?" Failure to recognize a complex question leads to all sorts of confusion in discussing an issue. Sometimes the complex question appears as a statement. Note the following resolution for a debate: *Resolved: That Congress should veto the inflationary budget proposed by the President.* Lurking behind this resolution are two separate resolutions: (1) that the budget proposed by the President is inflationary; (2) that the Congress should veto the budget.

The **excluded middle.** This is sometimes called the **either . . . or** fallacy or the **black and white** fallacy. "Either you support my proposal or you don't." Actually, we may support part of the proposal but not all of it. "Either we give criminals complete freedom or we give the police unlimited authority." There are degrees of freedom and degrees of police authority that the speaker is ignoring. We do not have to give criminals complete freedom nor do we have to give the police unlimited authority. This all-or-nothing fallacy reduces a situation to extremes. Slogans often employ this fallacy: America—Love It or Leave It. When Guns Are Outlawed, Only Outlaws Will Have Guns.

Pigeonholing. If we choose to, we can put our own slant upon almost any event. Some of us oversimplify a complex issue by stripping the issue of its complexities and by forcing that issue into some convenient general category. For instance, at a local university, Professor Reardon has published several scholarly articles in the past few years. A colleague remarks, "Reardon's always publishing. He must be a very frustrated person: I guess he's got to publish to keep himself occupied. There's something obsessive about the way he works. Poor guy . . . beautiful example of sublimation." At the same university is Professor Salers, who has never published. The same colleague remarks, "Salers never writes. I guess he just has nothing to say. He probably couldn't get published if he wanted to. Furthermore, he seems pretty lazy." You can't win: Damned if you do, damned if you don't.

One of the prime manifestations of oversimplification is **jumping to conclusions.** I remember once, having returned from a commercial laundromat, finding a pair of women's panties among my own laundered clothes. The panties had obviously been accidentally left behind by the person who had previously used the drier, and I had simply emptied the contents of the drier into my laundry bag. Well, I threw the panties into the wastebasket. A few minutes later, the thought occurred to me: What if I were to die now! What would people think, seeing a pair of women's panties in my wastebasket. I still chuckle at the speculations that that scene elicits.

The **fallacy of the beard.** What constitutes a beard? One whisker? No. Two whiskers? No. Three whiskers? No. Does the presence of one additional whisker make any difference? No. Obviously, there is no one place you can draw the line between having a beard and not having a beard. A person commits the fallacy of the beard when he argues that there is no distinction between two phenomena because there is no distinct point of demarcation between the two phenomena. This is a variation of the black and white fallacy. It manifests itself in various ways. (1) When a person says that one more won't make any difference. A school administrator says to a teacher, "Surely you can take one more student. One more isn't going to make any difference." Suppose that a few days later the administrator makes a similar plea ... and another one a few days after that. Now, it may be true that one more student will not make much of a difference, but there does come the point when the classroom is filled or when the class size is unmanageable. (2) When a person says that if A happens, then B will happen, and then C, and then D. "There's no drawing the line." This is the old **domino theory.** "If we allow City Hall to change the zoning regulations and permit a market on Winter Street, the next thing you know there'll be a McDonald's and we'll have a traffic mess and there'll be kids hanging around all the time making nuisances of themselves. And then they'll try to put in some chain store and then there'll be a shopping mall, and before you know it none of us will be able to live on Winter Street." (3) When a person uses the absence of clear-cut distinctions to rationalize inaction. Labor and management are disputing wages: "What is a fair wage? $2.00? "No." "$2.01?" "No." "$2.02?" "No." If management then argues that, since one additional cent isn't going to make any difference, they might as well discontinue haggling over pennies and stay with the *status quo*, then the management would be committing the fallacy of the beard.

Absolutes. People often indiscriminately use absolutes in their utterances: *every, everyone, everything, all, always, never, no one, nothing*. Rarely are these absolute terms justified. "No one likes the new tax proposal." "Everyone is dissatisfied with the mayor's proposal." In these statements *no one* and *everyone* really mean *most people* or perhaps even more precisely *most people that I have talked with*. Be leery of any statement that uses absolute terms.

The false mean. This is sometimes called the **fallacy of compromise.** Now, there are times when compromise is necessary. But it is not always a desirable solution. Sometimes an extreme positon is warranted. A doctor tells a patient who is now smoking two packs of cigarettes a day that he should stop smoking completely. "I'll tell you what, doctor," remarks the patient. "I'll cut down to a half pack a day." The patient's proposed compromise may help, but the doctor's original suggestion is better. One school administrator feels that all students should be required to take mathematics; another feels that no students should be required to take math. A compromise that only half the students be required to take math or that all students be required to take math for only two instead of four years is also unacceptable if, in fact, there is something intrinsically important about a four-year math program. A desirable solution does not always lie in compromise.

Circular definition. This fallacy is sometimes called a **question-begging definition.** You define a word so narrowly that it has to mean what you want it to mean: "You are a miser. As far as I am concerned, a miser is someone who is so tight that he won't take his wife to Europe on vacation. You won't take me to Europe this summer. You say that it's too expensive. That proves it: you're just a miser." The statement may be true according to the wife's definition, but only according to her definition. The husband is still not necessarily a miser according to the more universally accepted definition of the word.

Fallacy of the fall. "Ever since the fall of man in the Garden of Eden, man has been an imperfect being. Why try to improve the state of affairs! Man will just revert to his naturally corrupt instincts." The fallacy of the fall is an offshoot of the fallacies of equivocation and of accident. It is usually a type of rationalization for a person who doesn't want to be bothered or who doesn't want to take some decisive action. Example: There are two secretaries in an office, Gail and Gloria. Gloria constantly arrives late to the office. One day, Gail complains. The boss remarks, "Oh Gail, don't be too hard on Gloria. No one is perfect." Then, if the boss should remark that Gail too has her faults, he would be commiting the *tu quoque* fallacy.

Fallacy of reversion. "Why bother to repair the roads! They'll only fall into disrepair next winter and we'll just have to repair them all over again." This is another type of rationalization. People use this fallacy when they argue that it's a waste of time to do something because things will revert to their present state. Of course, this fallacy ignores that the present state, if it is not tended to, may get even worse.

Fallacy of time. "I agree that Mary has been hurt. But don't worry about it; she'll get over it. Time cures all wounds." "So the people in the suburbs are irate because we've reduced garbage collection. They'll get over it in time. Time will take care of everything." The problem here is that there is *some* truth to statements such as these. Time does have a way of tempering grievances. Still, it is irresponsible to rationalize taking no action by leaving matters up to time.

Fallacy of the worse evil, or the **resort to Pollyanna.** "So you broke your leg. Cheer up! Just think, you might have lost an eye instead." "So you wrecked the car; at least you didn't hurt yourself." "So you lost your job; at least your wife is still working." Such appeals are fallacious because they ask you to consider what might have been while depreciating what actually is.

Pollyanna is a novel by Eleanor Porter. The heroine, Pollyanna, is an excessively optimistic—comically optimistic—and naïve creature who could suffer no ill without finding some good in it.

Fallacy of determination. "Don't make excuses. If you really wanted to get here on time, you would have done so." "If you really wanted to lose weight, then you'd find a way to do so." "Where there's a will, there's a way." This fallacy suggests that anything is possible. If something that you would like to happen hasn't happened, the reason that it hasn't happened is that you haven't wanted it to happen strongly enough, i.e., you haven't tried hard enough to make it happen. The reason it hasn't happened is that you haven't been determined enough to make it happen. After all, claims this type of oversimplification, everything is possible if you just put your mind to it.

Fallacy of idealism. "You're approaching the problem all wrong. Don't threaten the students. Don't make a rule that says cheating is illegal and punishable by expulsion. Instead, meet with them and get them to realize that cheating in the long run will hurt only themselves. Then you won't need rules." "We can make it a much better world here if we just go about it the right way." "We shouldn't be thinking about the alcoholics. We should be thinking about the causes of alcoholism. If we can root out the causes of alcoholism, then we'll have really solved our problem." This type of glibness is used by those whose experience is limited and often by those whose lives have been sheltered. It is well-intentioned but hopelessly impractical. A more sensible approach to a complex problem is the one offered by Henry Peter Brougham on the subject of parliamentary reform. It is quoted by Jeremy Bentham in his *Handbook of Political Fallacies:*

> Looking at the House of Commons . . . my object would be to find out its chief defects and to attempt the remedy of these *one by one.* To propose no *system, no great project,* nothing which pretended even to the name of a *plan,* but to introduce in a temperate and conciliatory manner . . . one or two separate bills.

Fallacy of tacit agreement, or *argumentum ad quietem.* "No one is complaining; therefore, they are all content with the status quo." "No one disagreed; therefore, they all agree." The fact that you heard no dissent means neither that there is no dissent nor that the people are content. In a public meeting people may be reluctant to speak up for a variety of reasons. They may be shy; they may be afraid to make fools of themselves; they may be intimidated by other members of the group or by the presence of people in authority; they may be frustrated from previous unsuccessful efforts at speaking up; they may be temporarily awed by previous arguments and not know how to answer those arguments; they may not have sufficient facts to justify their beliefs; they may be unwilling to call attention to themselves.

The **false dilemma.** Many dilemmas reflect oversimplified thinking. Two extremes are presented as if they were the only alternatives when, in fact, there are actually several alternatives between the two extremes. The formula for a dilemma is

> If X is the case, then Y will occur.
> If A is the case, then B will occur.
> We have to choose between X or A.
> Therefore, Y or B will occur.

> If the students are honest, then we don't need an honor code.
> If the students are dishonest, then the honor code won't work.
> Students are either honest or dishonest.
> Therefore, either we don't need an honor code or an honor code won't work.
> Therefore, it's a waste of time to institute an honor code.

There are three ways of rebutting a dilemma. Sometimes all three will work, sometimes two of the three will work, and sometimes only one will work.

First, you can go *between the horns.* The *either . . . or* statement presents the horns of the dilemma, i.e., the alternatives. You show that reducing the argument to an *either . . . or* statement is inaccurate; you show that the two alternatives cited are not the only alternatives. In the above dilemma, you show that students are not either honest or dishonest but that there are degrees of honesty and dishonesty. "Therefore, we do not have to choose between X and Y."

Second, you can *grab one of the horns.* You take one of the *if* statements and show that it is not true. "If the students are honest, then we do need an honor code. It will encourage the honest students to exert a positive influence over the dishonest students." Or, "Your statement is not accurate. You can't talk about the students as if they were all alike. Some are honest and others are dishonest. An honor code will keep honest those who are now honest."

Third, you can present a *counter-dilemma*. You show that the components of the present dilemma can yield an entirely different conclusion:

If X is the case, then B will not occur.
If A is the case, then Y will not occur.
We have to choose between X or A.
Therefore, B or Y will not occur.

If the students are honest, then an honor code will work.
If the students are dishonest, then we need an honor code.
The students are either honest or dishonest.
Therefore, either an honor code will work or we need an
    honor code.
Therefore, we should institute an honor code.

The counter-dilemma does not *prove* that the dilemma is invalid. It merely illustrates that there is another way of looking at the situation.

Comparison and Contrast

*Logical consequences are the scarecrows of
fools and the beacons of wise men.*
Thomas Huxley, *Science and Culture*, ix

Devices of comparison and contrast can aid us in expressing ourselves. They add vividness and richness to our utterances, they are
sometimes a way of making concrete an abstract idea, and they
sometimes provide a means by which we can clarify a complex
idea.

For instance, students of geometry may find the following definition difficult to grasp: A *dihedral angle* is a set of points consisting
of the union of two intersecting half-planes and their common
edge. But if the students can picture two walls in a room that meet
each other and realize that the dihedral angle is the angle formed
by this meeting, the definition is much clearer.

Similarly, when the poet John Donne compares two people in
love to the legs of a drawing compass, his comparison allows him to
concentrate a complicated thought into just a few lines: Just as the
legs of a compass can be physically separated but are still always
joined by a common pivot, so two people in love cannot be truly
separated; they may be physically separated but they are still
joined by their souls or spirits, i.e., their love. They may be miles
away from each other, but their feelings for one another form a
spiritual bond that distance cannot affect.

Donne's comparison is an analogy, a comparison of two different things by showing the various ways in which those two things

are similar. The analogy, a means by which he can convey a complex thought, is entirely appropriate.

It is one thing to use an analogy to help to convey an idea. It is another thing to argue by analogy or to use an analogy to form an inference or judgment. Analogies are descriptive; they do not prove similarity. Furthermore, they only suggest similarity; they do not establish identity.

Analogies are abused when they try to claim similarity and to establish identity under the guise of merely suggesting that similarity. The following illustrations cite some of the ways that analogies are improperly used.

(1) An analogy compares X with Y. If X has the properties of *a,b,c,d,e,* and *f,* and if Y has the properties of *a,b,c,d,* and *e,* there is probably sufficient similarity to warrant a comparison. But sometimes there is not sufficient similarity. If X has the properties of *a,b,c,d,e,* and *f* and Y has the properties only of *b,d,* and *e,* then there is some similarity but not enough to argue that X and Y are similar. Example: Two admissions officers at a college disagree whether to accept Linda Standish into next year's freshman class. One admissions officer says to the other, "You have no right not to accept her. After all, you accepted Elizabeth Dorn. Both Standish and Dorn are honor students, both are females, both are good athletes. If you accept Dorn, then you have to accept Standish."

Now, there simply isn't enough similarity between the two girls to warrant the conclusion that Linda Standish and Elizabeth Dorn are equally qualified students. There are thousands of students who share these characteristics: female honor students who are also good athletes.

(2) Analogies are abused when there is significant dissimilarity that goes unnoticed. Let's continue the previous analogy. One admissions officer says to the other, "You have no right not to accept Linda Standish. After all, you accepted Elizabeth Dorn. Both Standish and Dorn are honor students; both are females; both are good athletes; both have college board scores in the seven-hundreds; both come from small rural communities; both are splendid musicians; one has had poetry published in a national magazine, the other won first prize at the all-state science competition; both have been leaders in extracurricular activities."

Now, there is indeed convincing similarity between the two

girls. The admissions officer does seem to have a strong argument. But, if he should ignore the fact that the hypothetical Linda Standish had been caught cheating three times during the past two years, his analogy would crumble. He would be ignoring a significant dissimilarity between the two girls.

(3) Analogies are abused when one particular similarity is used to equate two very different things:

"Now, don't be too hard on him. He meant well."
"Yeah, well, so did Hitler!"

Such an analogy is not only unfair; it's dirty. It creates a straw man and distorts the subject under discussion.

(4) Analogies are abused when a person uses the terms of one element to predict the terms of another element: "X has the properties of a,b,c,d,e, and f. Y has the properties of a,b,c,d, and e. Therefore, Y has the properties of f. This line of thought becomes particularly insidious when two people are being compared: Politician X has some qualities similar to Nixon's; therefore, X is another Nixon. Don't trust him.

When evaluating an analogy, ascertain answers to the following questions:

1. Have all the properties of X and all the properties of Y been cited?
2. How many of these properties are similar?
3. How many of these similarities are relevant?
4. To what extent are some of these similarities actually not as similar as they have been made out to be?
5. To what extent is X different from Y?

In challenging an analogy, try to find as many significant dissimilarities as you can. Try to show that many of the similarities are not significant or are irrelevant or are merely coincidental. And try to show that the dissimilarities outweigh and eclipse the similarities.

Previous chapters have suggested other types of improper comparisons. The metaphor, for instance (Chapter 6). A metaphor is a concentrated or implied analogy: "I resent the way he tried to weasel out of the agreement." There is an implicit analogy between the person and a weasel. The danger of metaphor is that it presents inference as if it were fact: "I interpret his actions as weaseling; therefore, he weaseled."

The use of statistics (Chapter 8) can lead to an improper comparison. Faulty or deceptive percentages: "Taxes have almost doubled under the present administration." But the present administration has been in office for sixteen years, during which time taxes in most other communities have tripled. The comparison between the boons of the previous administration and the horrors of the present administration distorts the truth of the situation.

Sometimes a comparison or contrast is simply invalid. Suppose someone tries to compare the conditions of a particular city to the conditions that he remembers thirty years ago. The comparison simply isn't fair. Times have changed so significantly in the past thirty years that trying to compare the two is meaningless. A mother says to her seventeen-year-old son, "How dare you challenge what I am saying. Just five years ago you would never have thought of challenging me." The claim may be true, but it is also both irrelevant and unfair. The standards of behavior of a seventeen year old are different from those of a twelve year old. The mother is not recognizing that the boy is now five years older and cannot be expected to follow the same rules of behavior that he followed five years ago. She is committing the **fallacy of irrelevant contrast.** And, if from this contrast she were to argue that her son has gone from good to bad, she would be committing the **fallacy of invalid contrast.**

An invalid contrast sometimes tries to compare apples with oranges, i.e., it tries to compare two items that are significantly dissimilar or it tries to use criteria that are inappropriate. "It's sheer nonsense to say that labor unions can hold their own against big business. Just General Motors or Xerox or Gulf and Western has more money than all the unions put together." The statement may be true, but the contrast is irrelevant. A union derives the most significant share of its power from its ability to bargain and from the number of members it contains, not from the amount of money that it has.

Another type of invalid contrast is illustrated by the following: "If young people have fresh and exciting ideas, then old people have stale and dull ideas." The thought process goes something like this: If X is associated with Y, then the opposite of X must be associated with the opposite of Y. This type of oversimplification is, of course, nonsense. It assumes that X and only X is associated with Y; therefore, anything that is not X cannot be associated with Y.

Another variation: "If they can put a man on the moon, why can't they stop inflation?" or "If they can develop the neutron bomb, why can't they come up with a way to cure cancer?" The ability to do one thing does not predicate the ability to do everything. This fallacy is a variation of the fallacy of composition. It assumes that if you can perform one significant deed, you can perform other significant deeds. This fallacy also implies another. It implies that they haven't bothered to try to stop inflation because they've been too busy putting a man on the moon; they have given so much of their energy to developing the neutron bomb that they haven't bothered much with cancer. It implies that science is more interested in making bombs than in finding a cure for cancer. And it even suggests that if scientists had tackled the problem of cancer with the same determination that they tackled the neutron bomb, then they could?/would?/might? have found a cure for cancer.

Still another variation: "What do you mean by saying that you do not want the police to have more power? What are you, against law and order?" "What do you mean by saying that the President shouldn't be able to declare war by *fiat?* What are you: some kind of Commie?" This type of unfair contrast creates a straw man and uses that straw man to try to vilify you. It is an example of arrant distortion. Consider this illustration: [1]

> The use of chemical pesticides for mosquito control is highly controversial. The poisons "kill mosquitoes efficiently [but they also] kill mosquito predators even more efficiently. Only the hardiest and most resistant mosquitoes survive the chemical blitz, and these impart a new genetic vigor to the following generation of mosquitoes which then explodes into a predator-free environment." Furthermore, these pesticides damage fish and wildlife, sometimes harm personal

1. Paraphrased from "Project Mosquito!" by Ted Williams, *New England Magazine (Boston Sunday Globe)*, July 2, 1978.

property, and sometimes "represent a threat to human health."

When a group of people began resisting the Massachusetts Reclamation Board's practice of indiscriminately spraying with these chemicals, the chairman of the Reclamation Board, replied:

> There's an organized group down there that is anti-mosquito-control. It's a group that's not representative of the taxpayers. I don't mean they're not taxpayers . . . Essentially they're trying to destroy the mosquito-control project.

Of course, this is nonsense. Not only nonsense but arrant distortion! The group is not against mosquito-control. It is against the dangerous and indiscriminate use of chemical pesticides. The thinking of people like the chairman is something like this: "If you don't want to do it my way, then you don't want to do it at all. If you don't want to do it, then you're against it. You don't want to do it my way; therefore, you're against it." Marvelous oversimplification but terrible logic.

The final fallacies presented in this chapter are **fallacies of consistency**. The abuse of consistency takes two different shapes; *the denial of the need of consistency* is the first. Mr. Edwards says to Mr. Kolb, "Hold on, you've just changed your position. Five minutes ago you were saying that the mayor's actions were deplorable. Now you're saying that his actions really weren't all that bad. Would you please make up your mind and adopt a more consistent position!" Mr. Kolb replies, "Consistency, baloney! Consistency is just the hobgoblin of little minds." Mushbrained people have used Mr. Kolb's line for years. You'll want to remember that if a person can change his mind every few minutes, he probably doesn't have much of a mind.

The second fallacy is the *false demand for consistency*. There are situations when the demand for consistency is foolish. When circumstances change, one's position must adapt. If I supported Nixon in 1968 and called him a scoundrel in 1973, I am not being inconsistent. So much has happened in the five years that my former position is no longer a relevant one.

There is nothing intrinsically wrong with the use of a comparison or a contrast. The danger occurs when the comparison or contrast is regarded as an end in itself, when a person attempts to imply identity instead of similarity, when the so-called similarity isn't in fact similar, and when the comparison or contrast is used to trigger the emotions and thereby to suspend reason.

"Remember Sacco and Vanzetti!" says a person inveighing against capital punishment.

"Just another Vietnam," says a person who disagrees with the government's decision to send military assistance to Israel.

"Just like Robin Hood—Steal from the rich and give to us poor!" claim a group of ghetto kids as they loot a local market.

"Police don't have guns in England; they shouldn't have them here. If it'll work in England, it'll work here."

"This perfume will grab and bowl him over," says Alice. "So will a skunk," replies her spiteful roommate.

"You're just another Brutus," says Harold to Horatio after Horatio refuses to lend money to Harold so that Harold can get a fix of heroin.

All of these statements are nonsense.

Evasion

*No one means all he says, and yet very few
say all they mean, for words are slippery and
thought is viscous.*
Henry Adams,
The Education of Henry Adams, xxxi

Evasion techniques are common. People use them to avoid a particular issue or charge, to avoid rigorous thinking and analysis, to camouflage complacency and glibness, and to avoid committing themselves to a particular position, belief, or attitude.

Several of the devices mentioned in earlier chapters can be used to evade. You can use many of the diversionary tactics mentioned in Chapter 9, you can respond ambiguously, or you can talk around the question without ever actually answering it.

A favorite technique is the **half-truth.** This technique was labeled the *fallacy of selection* in the suggestibility chapter. You answer a question by interpreting the words of that question literally, disregarding the spirit of the question. "If you've finished your homework, you can help me straighten out the house," a mother says to her son. "I haven't finished yet," says the son. The truth is that he has one more paragraph to read. But he is not telling a literal lie; he is merely not telling the whole truth. Furthermore, when he does finish that paragraph, he stays in his room, making no effort to help his mother. "After all," he rationalizes, "she didn't say 'When you finish your homework, please help me'; all she said was, 'If you've finished your homework, you *can* help me.'" The mother's sentence was a request couched as a statement. Literally, however, it was only a statement. The son has avoided doing something he doesn't want to do by ignoring the spirit of his mother's words.

You can avoid committing yourself to a position by **answering a question ambiguously.** You are asked, "Would you say that Paula Salter is honest?" Answer 1: "I have never known her to be dishonest." You respond to a question by answering the opposite of that question. Answer 2: "I have never *known* her to be dishonest." Or, "*I* have never known her to be dishonest." You use the technique of accent to suggest and insinuate an element of doubt without ever actually articulating that doubt. Answer 3: "Well, that's a tough question. It all depends upon how you define *honest.*" A nit-picking answer, probably designed to sidetrack the specific question but again implying some element of doubt without actually ever articulating that doubt. Answer 4: "She has always been a conscientious person whose loyalty to the company is without question." You simply avoid the question. Answer 5: You smile and perhaps laugh feebly. "Well, I wouldn't play poker with her. She's a mean poker player." You imply that her ruthless approach to poker is similar to her approach in other areas, but you do so under the guise of humor.

In each of these answers you have said nothing to incriminate yourself or to disparage Paula Salter. It's what you haven't said that is significant. In fact, almost any answer other than an enthusiastic yes is likely to suggest some element of doubt concerning Paula Salter's honesty.

You can evade a specific question by camouflaging your answer. A friend of yours asks you the specific question: "Do you like my latest poem?" You don't want to say no, and possibly hurt your friend's feelings. At the same time, you cannot in good conscience say yes. Perhaps you don't understand the poem; perhaps you haven't read it carefully enough; perhaps you actually do not like it. Therefore, you answer in one of the following ways:

"It was very interesting."
"I particularly liked the sound effects you used in the third stanza."
"It reminded me of T. S. Eliot's 'Wasteland.' "
"It was quite impressive."

If your friend does not pursue your answer, you're off the hook. Each of the above four answers suggests a *yes* answer to your friend's question without ever actually articulating that answer.

Here are some of the other stock lines and techniques used by people who wish to be evasive:

"Let's wait for a while and see what happens." Jeremy Bentham in his *Handbook of Political Fallacies* called this the **procrastinator's argument:** "Wait a little, this is not the time." His explanation is lucid: "This is the sort of argument which we so often see employed by those who, being actually hostile to a measure, are afraid or ashamed of being seen to be so. They pretend, perhaps, to approve of the measure; they only differ [they claim] as to the proper time to bring it forward. But only too often their real wish is to see it defeated forever."

"Let's just take **one step at a time;** we don't want to move too quickly all at once." This line may be fine as long as you're not faced with a serious situation that needs immediate and decisive attention.

"There are **too many ifs** involved; we'd better not chance it." There is nothing necessarily unsound with this line, but it should be examined carefully. Just what are the consequences of taking no action? Just what are these *ifs*, and how serious are they?

If we do A, then B will happen. If B happens, then C will happen. If C happens, then D will happen..." The old domino theory appears again. Such a projection may or may not present an accurate picture. The domino theory should be regarded circumspectly, for it often constitutes a sham attempt to predict the future.

A group of legislators are trying to determine what the quota on foreign oil imported into the United States should be. One legislator responds, "This whole discussion is missing the point. We shouldn't be talking about quotas and foreign oil. We should really be talking about improving our own energy sources. We should be talking about coal. We have enough coal in the United States to supply energy for the next century." And he continues to plead the case for coal. He has introduced a red herring. The issue under discussion is foreign oil, not coal. Coal may be an important topic, but not at this time. The subject of coal should be reserved for a separate discussion.

People will sometimes try to avoid the sting of a particular charge by **changing the words** of that charge. Sam says to Pete, "You did a terrible thing when you fired Ben Silver." Pete replies, "I did not *fire* Ben Silver. I merely suggested to him that it would be better for him if he were to move on, and I merely did not renew his contract." What Pete is forgetting or choosing to ignore is that, just as a rose by any other name is still a rose, so a spade by any other name is still a spade. Changing the language does not change the act.

Then there are **arguments of tradition and precedent:** "Well, we've always done it this way; I don't see why we should change now." "It's always worked in the past; we'd better leave well enough alone." What was appropriate for the past may not be appropriate for the present. The passage of time predicates change. A blind adherence to the past ignores this change. "We've never done it this way. Why start now?" The answer may be that the proposed way is better. Bentham is convincing on this point. "If the lack of a precedent presents a conclusive objection against the particular measure in question, so it would against any other measure that was ever proposed. This includes every measure that has ever been adopted, and so with every institution which exists at the present time. If the argument proves that this ought not to be done, it proves that nothing else ought ever to have been done." This is not to say that precedent should be ignored; it is only to say that it should be questioned and that its relevance to the present situation should be examined.

Just as there are people who blindly and uncritically fall back upon tradition and precedent, so there are people who blindly and uncritically scorn tradition and precedent. "We've been doing it this way for too long: it's time for a change." This is the *change for change' sake* argument. Change does not predicate improvement. New is not necessarily better.

The unquestioning appeal to, or scorn of tradition and precedent is a type of oversimplification and invariably reflects glib, shoddy thinking.

Finally, one can appear to answer a question by either overtly or tacitly **rephrasing that question** and then answering one's rephrased question.

Question: Should we allow girls to play football as part of the school's interscholastic athletic program?

MR. HALE: Well, only six girls have expressed an interest in football. Now, Sarah is much too weak for football. Louise has a part time job and won't have time. Edna is a good soccer player— she should stick with soccer. Caroline doesn't really seem to be all that interested; I think she's just going along with the other girls. . . .

Comment: Mr. Hale doesn't answer the question. The question entails a matter of principle and policy. Hale here avoids this issue by rephrasing the question to mean, "Is it practical for any of those girls who have expressed an interest in football to be allowed to play football?"

MRS. IVERS: Well, we don't have any football equipment for girls.

Comment: Again, the answer is irrelevant. First the school must decide whether it philosophically believes in girls' football. Then it can worry about ancillary concerns.

MR. JACKS: I don't know what this fuss is all about. There are only six girls who are interested, and we can certainly mollify them.

Comment: True, but that's not the point. The issue is not these six girls, although these six girls may have initiated the issue. We're talking about a matter of principle; the decision will have a long-range effect upon the school's athletic program.

MRS. KAHN: I don't see why we don't first initiate a cross-country program. Cross-country running is a wonderful sport. It's inexpensive, safe, and one gets splendid exercise.

Comment: Mrs. Kahn's comments are irrelevant. Cross-country running is a separate issue. Furthermore, did anyone say that, if the school admits football into its women's athletic program, it will not admit cross-country? Did anyone say that it is an either/or situation?

Question: Should the federal government give money to Chicago so that Chicago won't have to declare bankruptcy?

MR. PARRY: Well, of course, if we do bail them out, we'll get a good deal of good will from the Illinois voters. On the other hand, we'll lose votes from Indiana, since we cancelled the research grants to the University of Indiana, and Indiana is bound to think us unfair. On the other hand, if Chicago goes bankrupt . . .

Comment: Mr. Parry is avoiding the question by itemizing the pro's and the con's of the situation. He is straddling that proverbial fence and not committing himself.

MRS. QUINT: The federal government shouldn't deal directly with cities. That's the job of the state governments, it seems to me . . . besides, they're always accusing the government of infringing upon states' rights.

Comment: Mrs. Quint uses the reverse strategy of Mr. Hale's in the previous example. She uses a generality to answer a specific question. Her answer implies the fallacy of accident. She doesn't come right out and say, 'No, we shouldn't.' Instead, she twists the question to mean, 'Should the federal government give money to *cities* as a matter of policy?'

MR. ROLFE: Well, let me answer the question this way. Chicago got into this situation through carelessness and mismanagement and there's no sign that the same thing won't happen again.

Comment: Again, more evasion. He doesn't answer the question. Instead, he rephrases the question to mean, 'Why did it happen and can it happen again?'

MRS. SANDERS: Well, let me put it this way, what will happen if we don't bail out Chicago?

Comment: Is this a rhetorical question, is this ignorance parading as profundity, or is this simply a counter-question?

It isn't hard to be straightforward and to respond directly and firmly to a situation. But it does require that we know what we are talking about, that we have given some thought to the matter and are not responding off the top of our head, that we are not afraid to take a stand and to commit ourselves, that we detach our hobbyhorses and our biases from the topic under discussion, that we listen to what other people are saying, and that we honor the spirit as well as the letter of the question.

On Arguments

*It is possible to achieve mastery of a problem
or a skill without hurting another person or
even without attempting to conquer.*
Elliot Aronson, *The Social Animal,*
Chapter V.

It would be naïve to believe that arguments always occur in a spirit of honest inquiry. Some, perhaps many, do. But there are many other motivations that prompt people to argue. Therefore, when you find yourself in an argument, the first question you should ask yourself is "Why am I arguing?" and you should try to ascertain the motivation of your opponent.

Here are some of the reasons that people argue:

1. To get attention.
2. To show off or to impress others.
3. To compensate for weaknesses or frustrations.
4. To try to secure one-upmanship over another person.
5. To try to impose their will or ideas over others.
6. As an outlet for frustration or tension or hostility.

These six reasons, by no means discrete or inclusive, are personal reasons. An individual arguing for any of these motivations may not be seeking the truth, may not be interested in determining a reasonable course of action, and may not truly be eager to secure a resolution of the issue under discussion. Instead, it is the actual act of arguing that is important, not the outcome. Arguments of this type usually ramble, go off on all sorts of tangents, and are filled with much irrelevancy and often with much heated emotion. There is often considerable hyperbole, overreaction, and confusion. The twelve interferences cited in Chapter 4 frequently appear. But such unprofessional techniques are to be expected; after all, such arguments are not genuine ones. The personalities of the participants, not the outcome, is what is at stake. There is rarely a harmonious conclusion or resolution to such arguments; usually they just stop. These disputes are a form of play, sometimes aggressive play.

How do I want this argument to end? Do I want to get my opponent angry? So angry that he will storm out of the room? Am I actually looking for a fight? Do I want my opponent to lose his temper or to take a punch at me? Do I merely want to tease him? To embarrass him? To shake his complacency? To make him squirm? Do I just want to assert some superiority over him? Do I want to impress him (or the other people who are witnessing the argument) with my wit or my erudition or my cleverness or my naughtiness or my boldness or brazenness? Am I simply in a bad mood and see this argument as a way of letting off steam? Have I been put down today and now want to put someone else down? In other words, is it really the topic of the argument that I care about?

These are questions well worth considering when you find yourself entering an argument. They can be summarized: How do I want this argument to end? And what do I want to get out of this argument?

Many arguments are merely academic: Regardless of the outcome of the argument, that outcome will have no effect upon the topic. If people are disputing whether the Congress should approve the President's proposed anti-inflation legislation or whether the government should or should not have supported the actions of some foreign country, there is nothing to be gained. Their ultimate resolution, if there is one, will have no impact upon the Congress or upon the government.

But what about real arguments, the type that can have concrete results, the type used when parties are sincerely interested in resolving an issue, in securing a harmonious conclusion, and in solving a problem, i.e., the type of argument in which the prime concern is the outcome and the consequences of the outcome, not the personalities of the participants? Let us say that the emotional interferences cited in Chapter 4 are being avoided. How can the various parties proceed in ways that will be constructive and productive? First, let's take a look at the shape of a typical argument:

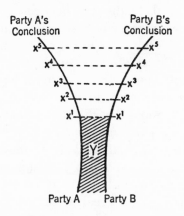

I am Party A and you are Party B. The first thing we should do is to clarify the nature of our argument: What specifically are we arguing about? What is the specific nature of our disagreement? What type of resolution are we seeking?

Next we should determine our common ground: the extent to which we agree. The cross-hatched area Y in the diagram represents common ground. In almost every disagreement, there are some points upon which both parties agree. Before we argue our disagreements, we should identify as specifically and as thoroughly as we can the points upon which we do agree.

The third step is to identify the first precise point of disagreement: Where does agreement stop? Where exactly do we *begin* to disagree? This is the line x^1 in the diagram. This may be the most difficult step in our procedure, but it is important because it allows us to pinpoint the first source of disagreement.

As we continue, we should try to identify and to resolve separately, one by one, each of the specific sources of disagreement. We should not talk about x^2 until we have resolved x^1. Above all, we should not argue the conclusions until we have identified, argued, and resolved each of the steps leading to the conclusion.

The goal of the argument is to remove as much of the distance as possible between the conclusion of Party A and the conclusion of Party B. This distance can be closed through compromise, each of the two sides giving a bit of ground here and there. It can be closed through conversion, one party being won over to the other party's point of view; even when conversion is achieved, the process may be a give-and-take one on each side. Of course, sometimes neither party gives ground, and the distance between the two conclusions is not closed; then we have a stalemate, and it may be fruitless for each of the two parties to persist in their disagreement.

Discussions often break down because people do not recognize what they are arguing about. They may each be talking about different issues or responding to different motivations. One person may be making assumptions that the other person isn't making and isn't recognizing. One party may not be expressing himself with sufficient clarity. The participants may be confused, and the precise issue at hand may have become lost. They may not be articulating their true motivation. For instance, a person criticizing an anti-contraception attitude may not realize that his true motivation is a personal one, perhaps even a selfish one: He engages in contraception and unconsciously regards any criticism of contraception as a threat to his behavior. The true issue then, the real bottom line, is not contraception as a matter of principle; it is his own personal behavior, which he must be able to defend to himself although not to others.

In order to avoid misunderstanding, arguers should clarify answers to the following questions:

A) Exactly what is the issue at hand?
B) Exactly what are we arguing about?
C) What type of resolution are we seeking? (How can we each get satisfaction?)
D) What are the facts?
E) To what extent do we agree?
    1. Do we agree on the facts? All of them? To what extent?
    2. Do we agree in our interpretation of the facts?
    3. Do we agree in our attitude toward the facts?
F) To what extent do we disagree?
    1. On what facts do we disagree?

2. Is our disagreement based on our separate opinions?
3. Are we confusing fact with opinion, speculation, or projection?

Then there are other points to keep in mind if we are really after a harmonious conclusion or resolution:

G) Try to maintain an equilibrium among the parties. Each of the arguers should always feel equal. Therefore, the person who has the strongest arguments may find it worthwhile to exert keen tact and delicacy and not to flaunt his strong position, for if he becomes too arrogant or self-righteous, he may run the risk of alienating his opponent(s).

H) Try to give the other person a way out; try to make a victory gentle and inconspicuous. Similarly, don't make the other party lose face.

I) Be sure not to confuse description with judgment. If you make a descriptive statement that might be regarded as judgmental, clarify that you do not intend to imply any judgment whatsoever. And when your opponent makes a similar statement, ask him whether his tone is judgmental or merely descriptive.

J) Be sure that the language is clear. When a vague or abstract word is used, be sure that its meaning is specified. Use language that is as concrete as possible.

K) Don't grope for arguments. Some people, especially when they have a vested interest in the outcome of a particular issue, will use any arguments they can think of to support their point of view. They will overstate, they will oversimplify, they will use faulty analogies or rely on faulty precedents not realizing that a poor argument is sometimes worse than no argument at all. When poor arguments are used, people who are neutral may become alienated while people who originally disagree will only disagree more. The only people who support specious arguments are those who already agree, and there is nothing to be gained by appealing to them.

L) Know when to stop. There is nothing to be gained by making an angry person even angrier. Similarly, recognize when the discussion is getting heated and try to cool that heat. Also, determine whether your opponent is listening to you or not. If he is not listening, if he is not about to respond to reason, then it may be fruitless to continue the discussion.

M) A key word is *clarity*. For instance, clarify inferences. Ask specifically, "Are you saying/suggesting/implying that . . ." Try tacks such as these:

—"All right. I understand your position. You want . . . Now, if you want to me accept your position, here is what you have to do. Can you do it?"

—"All right. You know what my position is: namely that . . . Now, what would I have to do to get you to accept my position?"

—"All right. We know each other's position. Now, what would you say would be a fair resolution to this issue?"

—"Do you recognize anything valid in my position? If you were I, how would you resolve this issue?"

To argue effectively requires skill, patience, delicacy, tact, diplomacy, sensitivity; it asks us to put aside our personalities and to address the issues; it requires us to be methodical, objective, analytic, and, above all, clear. It invites us never to make assumptions or inferences unless we clarify those assumptions or those inferences. And it especially insists that we do not begin with the conclusions but rather with the various steps that lead to the conclusions.[1]

1. For a very fine and thorough treatment of the nature and process of argument, I strongly recomment *Argument: An Alternative to Violence* by Abne M. Eisenberg and Joseph A. Ilardo, published (1972) by Prentice-Hall, Inc., Englewood Cliffs, New Jersey.

Some Nonsense: A Quiz

But now I'm going to be immoral; now
I mean to show things really as they are,
Not as they ought to be: for I avow,
That till we see what's what in fact, we're far
From much improvement with that virtuous plough
Which skims the surface, leaving scarce a scar
Upon the black loam long manured by Vice,
Only to keep its corn at the old price.

Byron, *Don Juan*, XII, xl

This is a good time to take a break and try a quiz. The following excerpts come from national magazines and newspapers, television and radio broadcasts, and personal experience. Evaluate each excerpt for its nonsense quotient. (The comments at the end of the quiz are by no means exhaustive.) Then continue the game by noticing letters to the editor in magazines and newspapers that you read, listening to comments on talk shows, noticing commercials and advertisements, and evaluating statements made in articles and newscasts. In fact, you might put a penny into a pot every time you hear an example of nonsense. You will run out of pennies before you run out of nonsense.

1. "Delta is ready when you are." (i.e., Delta Airlines)

2. (The setting is winter, Seattle, Washington. Four passengers are in a car. One asks another not to smoke in the car. The other's response:)

"Stop making such a fuss. You reformed smokers are all alike. You're always trying to remind people that you were able to quit."

3. (Setting: A public official of a major city reacting to a strike of the city's transit workers:)
"They're just a bunch of blackmailers, kidnapping hundreds of thousands of innocent commuters to extort some more money for themselves."

4. "If we don't save energy now, then fifty years from now there won't be any."

5. A darkhorse political candidate who campaigned loudly for tax reduction beats the favored candidate and ascribes his victory to
"The tidal wave of tax revolt."

6. "Everything tastes better with Blue Bonnet on it." (i.e., Blue Bonnet margarine)

7. "Abortion represents the ultimate in child abuse, the exploitation of women and escapism. Since we live in a society that excels in all three categories, it is not surprising that many of our citizens consider abortion to be a logical solution to an inconvenience."

8. (Setting: In the winter of 1977, a California doctor, who had unsuccessfully given an abortion to a young woman, was accused of strangling the baby when the girl gave birth to a thirty-one week old fetus that showed some signs of being alive. The incident became a *cause célèbre* when the doctor came to trial in the spring of 1978. Here are two reactions to the story:)
a. "[The woman] wanted an abortion from [the physician]. She got what she wanted: a dead fetus. Her $17 million litigation against the doctor is ludicrous."
b. "After reading the account of the . . . case, I fail to understand why he, alone, is on trial. Are countless other physicians who perform abortions less guilty than this doctor?"

9. (Setting: In the spring of 1978, President Carter strongly sup-

ported the selling of $4.8 billion worth of U.S. jet fighters to Israel, Egypt, and Saudi Arabia. A response:)

"Because of a combination of Saudi oil blackmail and Carter/ Brzezinski shortsided appeasement policy and apologetic propaganda, the Saudis will now get their military jets. But what that country, which still publicly beheads men and stones women to death, really needs is a twentieth century criminal code and not the most advanced weaponry made by mankind today."

10. (A quip from *Time:*)

"U.S. Congressman from Arizona ... suggested that the Post Office should handle inflation: *"They wouldn't solve it, but they'd certainly slow it down."*

11. (A psychologist of New York University commenting on the widespread appeal of roller coasters and other thrill-rides at amusement parks:)

"They are a safe way of breaking free of the realistic limits and an adult way of letting go of one's parents."

12. "Unemployment—major illness—major repairs to your house or car. Or, on a happier note, your dream vacation—your new home—or your daughter's wedding. What do all these have in common? A good oldfashioned savings account which can help you survive the bad times and enjoy the good times even more. At Barrons Savings Bank, the savings account hasn't taken a back seat to all the gimmicks and so-called *innovations* you hear so much about today. It may sound a little bit oldfashioned, but the Barrons Savings Bank still feels that the savings account is the soundest investment you can make for your future. Barrons Savings Bank: it pays the highest interest rates allowed by law and all deposits are insured in full."

13. "I'm sorry I didn't write. I meant to. I just never got around to it."

14. PENTAGON SPOKESMAN: "You talk about inflation; you talk about overspending; you talk about wasting money. Don't talk about us. Look at the Department of Health, Education, and Wel-

fare. They spend $500 million a day. We spend $118 billion a year. If you really want to talk about expenditures, go to HEW."

15. (The following are responses to articles on Joseph Califano, the former head of HEW, among whose many goals was to curtail the amount of cigarette smoking:)

a. "I read with alarm about Joseph Califano, Jr. Aside from the fact that he is a reformed smoker, the only thing I see that qualifies him for his position as Secretary of Health, Education, and Welfare is pure ego and compulsive overworking. I was not at all impressed with this continuation of an American stereotype and think he's headed for a heart attack. Why can't these zippy executives get their work finished on a normal work schedule?"

(Note: the above writer is referring to the fact that Califano often put in a work day of twelve or more hours.)

b. "When you chose to repeat Califano's baseless charge that cigarette advertising is *designed to convince* [young people] *that smoking is glamorous, adult, and sexually attractive,* you helped to perpetuate a myth Califano should know is incorrect. Without qualification, we deny the truth of these accusations. Smoking is an adult custom. We do not want or seek youngsters as customers. Numerous studies of teen-age smoking motivation show that other factors, such as peer influence, rejection of authority and the social environment, not advertising, are the major contributing factors. One needs only to look at increased teen-age use of marijuana, for which there are no ads, to see the faulty logic in these irresponsible charges."

(Note: the above response was submitted by a member of The Tobacco Institute, Inc.)

16. (A response to an article about a twenty-four old man who is suing his parents "for the malpractice of parenting":)

"As long as we are suing our parents, let us all lodge a suit against Adam, the first of a long line of parents who did not know what they were getting into."

17. (Response to an article that described the glutted job market

faced by English and foreign language teachers; even Ph.D.s are struggling to find jobs:)

"It used to be that a person with a Ph.D. was one whose ability had been proved by the discovery of new knowledge or the successful defense of new ideas. How could 1,847 Ph.D. candidates in one year all discover new knowledge about English or languages, or develop new ideas and theories? The degree simply no longer means what it used to. Should its possessors expect to get what their predecessors did?"

18. (Advertisement for Cruzan Rum:)

THE BEST RUM UNDER THE SUN IS THE ONE MADE WITH RAIN

Rainfall in the Virgin Islands is rare. But it's precious. Not only for our greenery, but also for our rum.

Because before Cruzan reaches the peak of mellowness, we add a little rain to every barrel.

As a result, light-bodied Cruzan Rum is not only extremely smooth, it is exceptionally clean-tasting. As clean-tasting as the rain water it's made with.

19. (Advertisement for Haspel Bros., Inc., clothiers:)

"The seersucker suit: easy care summer wear..No one does it like Haspel."

20. "The college's athletic department should go after good athletes. The stronger an athletic team is, the better-off for the college. Like it or not, alumni follow our teams carefully. When a team has a winning season, the alumni are much more willing to send in donations, and when they send in donations, the whole school benefits. Furthermore, recruitment is a part of our world. When a company needs someone with a particular skill or talent, they go after that person. In the same way the athletic department should go after the best athletic talent. Just as this school strives for excellence, so do we want excellence on our teams."

21. "Only Brut gives you effective and long lasting protection plus the great smell of Brut."

22. (When the Surgeon General issued his second major report on smoking, Joseph Califano, former Secretary of Health, Education, and Welfare—himself an ex-smoker—wrote a strong foreword stressing the dangers of smoking. A spokesman for the tobacco industry remarked:)

"America beware if Joe Califano ever gives up drinking or other pleasure pursuits, even the most intimate."

COMMENTS ON THE NONSENSE EXAMPLES

1. An exaggerated claim. I called Delta to see whether they could take me to Seattle. They couldn't. They weren't ready when I was.

2. Wrong reason; reversal of cause and effect. Someone else's smoke can be downright obnoxious.

3. Straw man: oversimplification, overreaction, exaggeration, and distortion; emotional language; negative image words; name-calling; use of labels.

4. Will the sun be gone in fifty years? What the speaker means to say is something like this: "If we don't save energy now, then fifty years from now we may not be able to rely upon the same energy sources that we rely upon now." Even the restatement, however, is an oversimplified point: Suppose that we do save energy now; won't we just be postponing the inevitable? Is the issue the conservation of present energy sources or the development of new sources?

5. Our poor politician doesn't realize that tidal waves are destructive. A most unfortunate metaphor.

6. Ever try Blue Bonnet on your sherbet?

7. Straw man; question begging definition—in fact, a very bizarre definition of *child*. A fetus is not a child. One wonders, furthermore, how abortion is tantamount to the exploitation of women. Does our society, in fact, excel in child abuse? Does it excel in the exploitation of women? Does it excel in escapism, whatever *escapism* means? The whole response is a series of non sequiturs and is probably motivated by a very strong emotional and personal reaction of the writer.

8. Neither response is willing to acknowledge that there is a difference between abortion and murder or, perhaps more precisely, between aborting an embryo and actually strangling a baby.

9. The response is guilty of *either/or* thinking. It consists of a series of non sequiturs. What does their criminal code have to do with their building of a powerful air force? A nice example of illicit contrast.

10. Equivocation. The logic is something like this: The Post Office is slow: it slows down the mail; it is therefore good at slowing things down. Inflation needs to be slowed down. Therefore, the Post Office should be in charge of inflation.

11. Anyone who is tempted to say *nonsense* to this statement should be careful. Unless we are trained psychologists and know what we are talking about, we had better remain silent.

12. This pitch equates old-fashioned with good: because it's old-fashioned, it's therefore good. What are these gimmicks and innovations, and why are they a threat to a savings account? One wonders whether the bank isn't protesting too much, whether all this hubbub about the good old days isn't some sort of rationalization. Furthermore, given our inflationary economy, is it true that "the savings account is the soundest investment" a person can make for the future?

13. Translation: "I didn't feel like writing" or "Writing was very low on my list of priorities."

14. Confusing contrast: $118 billion a *year* vs. $500 million a *day;* invitation to pursue a red herring: The issue is the Pentagon; HEW is a separate issue.

15. Response *a* forgets that Califano doesn't have a *normal* job. Why should being a reformed smoker qualify him to be Secretary of HEW?

Does speaker *b* mean to suggest that smoking does *not* project an image of glamourousness, sophistication, and sexual attractiveness and that youth is *not* turned-on by such an image?

16. Straw man: *reductio ad absurdum.*

17. Translation: It is unlikely that all Ph.D.s have discovered something new or developed some new idea or theory. Therefore, all Ph.Ds have not discovered something new or developed some new idea or theory. Therefore, they don't deserve to have jobs. Response also confuses sufficient with contributory cause.

18. Translation: "Rain water is clean-tasting. We add a little rain water to every barrel of our rum. Therefore, our rum is made with rain. Therefore, our rum is clean-tasting." Why does adding a little rain to a barrel of rum make that rum clean-tasting? Is there some rum that isn't clean-tasting? If Cruzan Rum added tap water instead of rain water, would the rum cease to taste clean? Would it then taste dirty?

19. What is it that Haspel does?

20. Faulty analogy. The spokesman is forgetting that before a person can be recruited as an athlete, that person must first be a competent student. Spokesman is under the impression that the needs of the athletic department come first.

21. Circular reasoning here. All this statement says is that only Brut gives you the great smell of Brut. In no other way is Brut unique. The ad makes no claim about the uniqueness of Brut's protection. The use of the word *and* in this ad is clever and subtle.

22. An *ad hominem* attack, a mild appeal to humor (or perhaps sarcasm), and a reversal of cause and effect. The spokesman's reasoning goes something like this: The reason Califano is against smoking is that he himself is an ex-smoker. Consequently, if he ever quits drinking, he will find fault with that; and if he ever finds himself unable to engage in lovemaking, he will say that lovemaking is harmful.

Of course, the spokesman will not admit the possibility that Califano stopped smoking *because* it is dangerous.

Some Semantic Problems

"The remote source of his defeat lies in the supposition that the Minister is a fool because he has acquired renown as a poet. All fools are poets; this the Prefect feels; and he is merely guilty of ... thence inferring that all poets are fools."

Poe, *The Purloined Letter*

Now we'll continue the discussion begun in chapters 7 and 12; we'll deal with some specific problems in semantics, in deduction, and in reasoning.

We've already seen that individual words can be ambiguous because a speaker hasn't clarified which of the possible meanings he's using. This is called **semantic** or **verbal ambiguity.** *He caught a crab. Crab* can refer to the shellfish, or it can refer to a poor stroke in rowing. A clever aspirin slogan capitalized on the semantic ambiguity of the verb *catch:* "At the sign of a cold, use aspirin. Catch that cold before you catch cold." *She follows stars* can have at least three different meanings: (1) She is interested in the comings and goings of celebrities. (2) She accompanies celebrities as they come and go—for instance, a journalist who reports on celebrities. (3) She is interested in astronomy. A *radical solution* can be one that gets to the root of a problem or one that is extreme and daring or one that is to the far left-wing.

A word can be ambiguous because of its position in the sentence. Its syntax, i.e., its relationship to the other words in that sentence, is not clear. This is called **syntactic ambiguity,** or **amphiboly.**

The problem with Mr. Tarn is that he can't make decisions quickly enough on problems he doesn't understand.

We would indeed hope that Mr. Tarn does not make decisions on problems that he doesn't understand. The amphibolous sentence structure can be clarified:

The problem with Mr. Tarn is that there are too many problems he doesn't understand; consequently, he can't make decisions quickly enough.

Is a *smoking pipe* a pipe that is emitting smoke or a pipe for smoking? Is a *lightweight crew coach* a crew coach who isn't very effective or a coach of a lightweight crew? Is a *wild game warden* a game warden who is mad or a warden of wild game?

We have already seen that the words *because* and *so* can be ambiguous (Chapter 11). *Since* and *as* can cause similar problems, especially when they are used in an improperly phrased sentence.

Since the police have been given greater authority, crime has decreased.

Since can mean *because* or *ever since;* it can express a causal or merely a temporal relationship.

As I finished mowing the lawn, I had a beer.

The *as* in this sentence can mean *while* or *because.* In neither case, however, is the sentence grammatically accurate.

Conjunctions can pose a problem. Take the word **and.** It can express addition or equivalence. "This will be a chapter about confusion and inference" can mean "This will be a chapter about confusion and also about inference." But the sentence can also suggest a connection between confusion and inference. In other words, the phrase *confusion and inference* can be regarded as two separate phenomena or as one combined phemomenon. "Sarah and Miranda received an award last night" can mean that the two girls shared an award or that the two girls each received a separate award. Confusion can occur when a person uses *and* in such a way as not to make clear whether the word is expressing equivalence or merely addition.

There are other problems with the word *and.* Take this sentence: "I went down South during my vacation and visited my Aunt Nora." This sentence may merely be stating two unrelated events. But some people will use the word *and* to indicate purpose: "I went down South during my vacation to visit my Aunt Nora." Sometimes *and* assumes a temporal or a causal relationship. "Mr. Tull got sick and died" can mean "Mr. Tull got sick and then he died," "Mr. Tull got sick and as a result he died," "Mr. Tull died because of his illness."

Sometimes *and* means *both . . . and.* The Brut example used in the previous chapter nicely illustrates this use:

> Only Brut gives you effective and long-lasting protection plus the great smell of Brut.

This statement really means, "Only Brut gives you *both* effective, long lasting protection *and* the great smell of Brut." In order for the statement to be true, both of the statements joined by *and* have to be true. Thus, one cannot say, "Only Brut gives you effective and long-lasting protection." Brut is not the only deodorant that gives effective and long-lasting protection. But it is the only deodorant to combine long-lasting protection, effective protection, and the smell of Brut.

To make matters even worse, *and* can sometimes mean *or:*

> The following examples come from *Time, Life,* and *Newsweek.*

Each example doesn't come from all three magazines. Each example comes either from *Time* or from *Life* or from *Newsweek.* The sentence really means, "Some of the examples come from *Time,* others from *Life,* and others from *Newsweek."*

The word **both** can be ambiguous. When I say "Both handbrakes on my bicycle don't work," I can mean "One of the handbrakes doesn't work" (i.e., *"Both* don't work, just one works") or

"Neither handbrake works." Because of this potential ambiguity, it is a good idea to avoid the *both . . . not* pattern and instead to say either *one . . . not* or *neither.*

The same type of ambiguity appears with the pattern **all . . . not.**

 i) All Cadillacs are not made by American Motors.
 ii) All Cadillacs are not made in Detroit.

As long as one knows that Cadillacs are made by General Motors, and that General Motors is a separate company from American Motors, the meaning of the first sentence is clear: There are no Cadillacs made by American Motors. But look at the second sentence. Does it mean "There are no Cadillacs made in Detroit" or does it mean "Some Cadillacs are not made in Detroit?" In other words, "*All* Cadillacs aren't made in Detroit, just some of them." Again, it is a good idea to avoid the pattern *all . . . not* and instead to use the words *no* or *some . . . not.*

In fact, the problems with negatives are so important that a point made in Chapter 12 bears repetition: The statement "I am not with you" does not necessarily mean "I am against you." It merely means that I do not support you in what you are about to do. When I say "I don't like veal," I am not necessarily saying "I dislike veal." I am merely expressing a lukewarm attitude toward it. And when I say "I don't believe you," I am not necessarily saying that I disbelieve you. The expression *not-X* does not necessarily mean the opposite of X; it merely means the absence of X. "The water is not hot" doesn't necessarily mean that the water is cold; the water may be 70°, neither hot nor cold.

The word **or** is tricky. *Or* can have two different functions. It can be *inclusive,* as in the following sentence:

I am uncomfortable in very hot or in very cold weather.

In this statement, the *or* is actually equivalent to *and:*

I am uncomfortable in very hot weather and (I am uncomfortable) in very cold weather.

I am uncomfortable in both very hot and very cold weather.

On the other hand, *or* can be *exclusive:*

The keys are in the kitchen or in the bedroom.

In this statement, the keys may be in the kitchen and they may be in the bedroom, but they cannot be in both the kitchen and the bedroom.

Confusion can occur when a person uses *or* in such a way as not to make clear whether the inclusive or exclusive use of the word is intended.

A fallacy can occur when a person reasons that one of the alternatives is false because the other is true, i.e., when one assumes the exclusive meaning of *or* when the inclusive is intended.

Laura will pass her exams or she will leave law school.

It is incorrect to reason that because she left law school, she did not pass her exams. There are other reasons that might require her to leave law school. It is equally fallacious to reason that, because she passed her exams, she will not leave law school. On the other hand, it is valid to reason that if she doesn't pass her exams, she will leave law school, and that if she doesn't leave law school, she has passed her exams.

Therefore, it is invalid to say that, if one alternative is true, the other alternative is not true. But it is valid to say that, if one alternative is not true, the other is true. The following lists the valid and the invalid deductions that can be made from a statement with the word *or*. X and Y are the two alternatives.

Valid

Either X or Y is the case.	Either X or Y is the case.
X is not the case.	Y is not the case.
Therefore, Y is the case.	Therefore, X is the case.

Invalid

Either X or Y is the case.	Either X or Y is the case.
X is the case.	Y is the case.

Therefore, Y is not the case.   Therefore, X is not the case.

Of course, *the case* can be read as *true: X is the case* is the same as *X is true*.

One must be careful with the word *if*. Many people assume that *if* means *if and only if*. It doesn't. *If and only if* specifies and restricts the possibilities; *if* doesn't specify anything; it merely cites a condition. The following two statements are different:

I will stay home if it rains.
I will stay home only if it rains.

The second statement indicates that only one thing will keep me home: rain. The first statement, on the other hand, merely says that rain will keep me home; other things may keep me home too. It is fallacious to reason from the first statement that, if I am at home, then it is raining, or that I will not stay home if it doesn't rain, or that if it is not raining, then I am not at home.

Let us look more carefully at this word *if*. What can we validly deduce and where can our deductions go astray? We'll work with an easy example:

If Aunt Edna visits us, she will be treated well.

First, we can say that if she is not being treated well, then she is not visiting us. But, we cannot say that if she is being treated well, then she is visiting us. She could be being treated well by a host of other people. Nor can we say that if she is not here, she is not being treated well. Again, her being here is not the exclusive condition of her being treated well.

We commit a fallacy when we assume that the converse of a condition is true. The converse of *If X is true, then Y is true* is *If Y is true, then X is true*. The converse is not always true:

If you eat poison, you will die. —Statement
If you died, you ate poison.   —Converse

The *if* part of a condition is called the *antecedent;* the *then* part is called the *consequent.* Another name for the fallacy just described is the fallacy of *affirming the consequent*. You affirm the consequent when you say that, because the consequent is true, the antecedent must be true.

We commit another fallacy when we assume that the obverse of a condition is true. The obverse of the example above is, "If Aunt Edna does not visit us, then she is not being treated well." The obverse of *If X is true, then Y is true* is *If X is untrue, then Y is untrue.* The obverse of a condition is not always true:

If you eat poison, you will die. —Statement
If you don't eat poison, you won't die. —Obverse

Another name for this fallacy is *denying the antecedent*. You deny the antecedent when you say that because the antecedent is not true, the consequent is not true.

The following lists some of the valid deductions that can be made from an *if . . . then* statement. Again, the phrase *the case* can mean *true*. Thus, *If X is the case, then Y is not the case* can be read *If X is true, then Y is not true.*

Valid

If X is the case, then Y is the case.
X is the case.
Therefore, Y is the case.

If X is the case, then Y is the case.
Y is not the case.
Therefore, X is not the case.

If X is not the case, then Y is the case.
X is not the case.
Therefore, Y is the case.

If X is the case, then Y is not the case.
Y is the case.
Therefore, X is not the case.

If X is not the case, then Y is not the case.
X is not the case.
Therefore, Y is' not the case.

Invalid

If X is the case, then Y is the case.
Y is the case.
Therefore, X is the case.

If X is the case, then Y is the case.
X is not the case.
Therefore, Y is not the case.

If X is the case, then Y is not the case.
Y is not the case.
Therefore, X is the case.

The two invalid forms to the left affirm the consequent, or assume the converse. The invalid form to the right denies the antecedent, or assumes the obverse.

There is one final variation of the *if ... then* type of condition that is worth mentioning: the chain condition, sometimes called the serial or the hypothetical condition:

If the weather is good, I will set out tomorrow.
If I set out tomorrow, I will visit my sister.
If I visit my sister, I will spend the night in Milwaukee.
If I spend the night in Milwaukee, I will not stop off in Chicago.
Therefore, if the weather is good, I will not stop off in Chicago.

The pattern of such arguments is:

If A is the case, then B is the case.
If B is the case, then C is the case.
If C is the case, then D is the case.
If D is the case, then E is the case.

Given this pattern, the following are proper conclusions:

If A is the case, then C is the case.
If A is the case, then D is also the case.
If A is the case, then E is also the case.

and so on. But the chain condition is easily abused:

If you love your country, you will vote.
If you are interested in government, you will vote.
Therefore, if you love your country, you will be interested in government.

The pattern of this fallacious argument is:

If A is the case, then B is the case.
If C is the case, then B is the case.
Therefore, if A is the case, then C is the case.

Clearly, one can love one's country without being interested in government. Here is another type of fallacy:

If you want good government, you will attend City Council meetings.
If you want good government, you will support the Liberal Party.
If you attend City Council meetings, you will support the Liberal Party.

This argument may sound attractive, but it is not a valid one. Remember, in order for an argument to be valid, any terms must be able to be plugged into the formula. The formula here is:

If A is the case, then B is the case.
If A is the case, then C is the case.
Therefore, if B is the case, then C is the case.

The invalid form of this argument is exposed when a different set of terms are substituted:

If you are in Chicago, you are in the northern part of the U.S.
If you are in Chicago, you are in Illinois.
Therefore, if you are in the northern part of the U.S., you are in Illinois.

You can be in the northern part of the U.S. without being in Illinois. You might be in Seattle or Bangor.

Any argument that allows an untrue conclusion from two true statements is an invalid argument.

The chapter will close with two more semantic problems, the article *the* and the verb *to be*. **The** is a *definite* article. "The citizens of California are eager for tax reform." The problem, however, occurs when this article is loosely used as an indefinite article, as it so often is. The sentence just cited really means "Some of the people of California are eager for tax reform" or "Many of the people ..." or perhaps even "Most of the people ..." It is irritating to hear a person inaccurately assign the inclusive meaning to *the*. When a representative says, "The people in my district will not support this proposal," he really means, "Some/Many of the people in my district ..." or perhaps, even more to the point, "Some/Many of the people that I have talked with ..." There may be a significant difference between "The people" and "Some/Many of the people I have talked with."

I have saved discussion of the verb **to be** to the end because it is probably the least dangerous of the semantic problems mentioned in this chapter. This verb can have at least four different functions. It can designate *identity:* $X = X$. A taxicab is a taxi. The two are one and the same; the only difference is the name. We can interchange the words without affecting the meaning. The verb can also designate *equivalence, equality,* or *congruence:* $X \cong Y$. Suppose we have two different lines that have the same length and width or two pieces of a jigsaw puzzle that exactly duplicate each other. When we say that these two lines or these two pieces are equal, we do not mean that they are the same lines or the same pieces. All we mean is that they are duplicates of each other in size and shape. A third function of the verb *to be* designates *membership in a class:* $X \cong Y$. "Arsenic is a poison" means "Arsenic is a type of poison" or "Arsenic is a member of the class designated by the term *poison.*" We cannot interchange the two terms of the statement, *arsenic* and *poison.* Finally, the verb can designate *intersection:* $X \cap Y$. In this function, the verb means "to have at least one characteristic of." "Larry is a skunk" means "Larry has at least one of the qualities of a skunk." In other words, the qualities that Larry has and the qualities that a skunk has intersect or overlap at at least one point.

Some of the semantic problems mentioned in this chapter are

obvious ones. Others are more subtle. Even the most precise speaker will probably never completely avoid them all. But perhaps if we are alert to the pitfalls, we will be more careful to say what we mean.

21

The Syllogism

"Tell me some of your mistakes."

"I am almost ashamed," said Sissy, with reluctance. "But today, for instance, Mr. McChoakumchild was explaining to us about ... National Prosperity. And he said, Now, this schoolroom is a Nation. And in this nation, there are fifty millions of money. Isn't this a prosperous nation? Girl number twenty, isn't this a prosperous nation, and an't you in a thriving state?"

"What did you say?" asked Louisa.

"Miss Louisa, I said I didn't know. I thought I couldn't know whether it was a prosperous nation or not, and whether I was in a thriving state or not, unless I knew who had got the money, and whether any of it was mine. But that had nothing to do with it. It was not in the figures at all," said Sissy, wiping her eyes.

"That was a great mistake of yours," observed Louisa.

"Yes, Miss Louisa, I know it was, now. Then Mr. McChoakumchild said he would try me again. And he said, "This schoolroom is an immense town, and in it there are a million of inhabitants, and only five-and-twenty are starved to death in the streets in the course of a year. What is your remark on that proportion? And my remark was—for I couldn't think of a better one—that I thought it must be just as hard upon those who were starved, whether the others were a million, or a million million. And that was wrong, too."

Dickens, *Hard Times*, I, ix

We were introduced to the concept of arguments in Chapter 7. The most important points made in that chapter were—

1. An argument consists of a series of statements, or premises, from which is derived a conclusion.

2. An argument is *valid* if the conclusion incontrovertibly derives from the premises. It is *invalid* if the conclusion does not incontrovertibly derive from those premises.

3. An argument can be valid even if one or more of its premises are untrue. Truth and validity are two separate matters, each of equal importance. Validity applies only to the logic, or reasoning process, not to the truth of the statements.

4. Some arguments are *enthymemes,* i.e., incomplete: One or more of the premises are omitted. Sometimes these omitted premises are obvious; sometimes they are not obvious, at which point they are liable to lead to confusion and misunderstanding.

In logic, the nucleus of the reasoning process is the syllogism. A syllogism is a type of argument that consists of two premises and a conclusion. When one talks about syllogisms, one must consider both their form and their statements. For instance,

All dogs are beagles.
Baron is a dog,
Therefore, Baron is a beagle.

This is a perfectly valid syllogism even though the first statement is untrue. If that first statement were true, then the conclusion would have to be true. On the other hand, the syllogism

Some dogs are beagles
Baron is a dog.
Therefore, Baron is a beagle.

is invalid even though the premises are true. There is something wrong with the *form* of a syllogism if it permits untrue or faulty conclusions from true premises.

Therefore, when one evaluates a syllogism, one has to answer these two questions: (1) Is each of the two statements true? (2) Is the syllogism valid, i.e., is it set up correctly? This chapter will deal with some of the criteria by which you can distinguish a faulty (i.e., invalid) from a valid syllogism.

A proper syllogism contains three and only three terms. The *minor term* is the subject of the conclusion and it appears once in one of the premises; the *middle term* appears in each of the two premises but not in the conclusion; the *major term* is the predicate of the conclusion and it appears once in one of the premises.

A term can be singular in one of the three sentences and plural in the other. *A dog, some dogs, dogs, all dogs, no dogs* are all different ways of expressing the same term.

Thus, in the following syllogism

All dogs are canines.
This animal is a dog.
Therefore, this animal is a canine.

the major term is *canine,* for it appears as the predicate of the conclusion; the minor term is *animal,* for it appears as the subject of the conclusion; the middle term is *dog,* for it appears in each of the two premises but not in the conclusion.

Each term of a syllogism has a *quantifier:* the word *all* or *some* or *no.* Sometimes the word is not stated. For instance, the premise *Dogs are not reptiles* really means *No dogs are reptiles* or *All dogs are not reptiles. All* and *no* are called *universal* quantifiers since they say something about each and every member of the class denoted by the term. A term with *all* or *no* is called a *distributed* term. Proper nouns or their equivalents are regarded as universal/distributed even though the quantifier *all* is not expressed. Thus, in the statement *Harry is courteous, Harry* is regarded as distributed, or universal, since there is only one person that we are talking about. In the statement *This animal is a dog, this animal* is regarded as universal, or distributed, since we are referring to one and only one animal, i.e., a specific animal for whom a proper name could easily be substituted.

Some is a *particular* quantifier since it says something about only a *part* of the class denoted by the term. (Note that *particular* does *not* mean specific.) The word *some* merely means *one or more,* or *at least one.* Whereas a universal/distributed term is specific, a term with *some* is not specific.

A term with *some* is often called an *undistributed* term. Sometimes the word *some* is omitted. For instance, the sentence *All snakes are reptiles* says nothing about the whole race of reptiles; it merely says something about those reptiles that are snakes, i.e., that part of the reptile class occupied by snakes. In the statement *Sam is a dog,* the term *a dog* does not apply to the whole race of dogs; it merely says something about that part of the dog world occupied by Sam. Thus, in these two examples, *reptiles* and *a dog* are each particular or undistributed terms.

We can continue our study of the syllogism with two very easy criteria for validity. First, if either of the premises begins with *some,* the conclusion must also begin with *some.* Secondly, if there is a negative in either of the premises, there must be a negative in the conclusion.

All dogs are canines.   All dogs are canines.
Tabby and Daniel are not   Some dogs are gentle.
    dogs.   Therefore, . . .
Therefore, . . .

The first syllogism must have a conclusion phrased in the negative: "Therefore, Tabby and Daniel are not canines." The second syllogism must have a conclusion that begins with *some:* "Some canines are gentle." In the following syllogism

Some dogs are gentle.
No dogs are reptiles.

the conclusion must combine the *some* with the negative: Some . . . not . . . : "Therefore, some gentle things (animals, creatures) are not reptiles."

The next two criteria are equally easy: No conclusion can be derived from two premises beginning with *some* and No conclusion can be derived from two negative premises.

Some girls are attractive.
Some girls are tall.

There is nowhere you can go, given these two premises.

No cats are canines.
No reptiles are cats.

It may be tempting to try the conclusion: "Therefore, no reptiles are canines." The statement is true, but it is not a valid deduction. Remember, in order for the form of a syllogism to be valid, it has to be valid for any terms that are plugged into it. Examine the slight substitution:

No cats are canines.
No dogs are cats.
Therefore, no dogs are canines.

Any syllogism whose premises are true but whose form allows the conclusion *No dogs are canines* has to be a worthless syllogism. It is clearly an invalid syllogism.

In syllogisms in which the premises are both affirmative (i.e., in which there are no negatives), the major term denotes a class, the middle term a subclass, and the minor term a sub-subclass or a specific within that subclass. For instance,

All cats are felines.
Daniel is a cat.
Therefore, Daniel is a feline.

P = felines, a class: the major term.

M = cats, a subclass, a type of feline: the middle term.

S = Daniel, a sub-subclass of cats, a specific cat: the minor term.

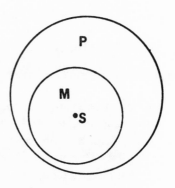

We have already seen what can happen in affirmative statements when the middle term is not a true middle (p. 109):

A dog is a canine.
A wolf is a canine.
Therefore, a wolf is a dog.

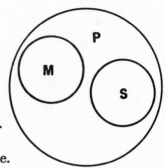

P = canines, a class: the major term.

M = dogs, a subclass, a type of canine.

S = wolves, a subclass, a type of canine.

This type of fallacy occurs when people regard two different things as equivalent just because the two things have some common characteristic or just because they belong to the same class. The danger of this fallacy is that it is sometimes subtle:

Anarchists are people who are dissatisfied with the government.
Harry is dissatisfied with the government.
Therefore, Harry is an anarchist.

P = people who are dissatisfied with
        the government, a class

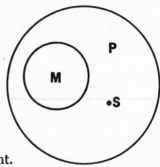

M = anarchists, a subclass, a type of
        person dissatisfied with the
        government.

S = Harry, a specific person who is
        dissatisfied with the government.

Now, this syllogism would appear to be valid. After all, we have a class, a subclass, and a specific. The fallacy is that the premises do not state that the specific (Harry) is a member of the subclass (anarchists). Therefore, there is no true middle. The fallacy becomes even clearer when we substitute *human* as the major term:

Anarchists are human.
Harry is human.
Therefore, Harry is an anarchist.

The fact that Harry and anarchists have some common qualities—they are human; they are dissatisfied with the government—does not mean that we can equate or even identify them.

Furthermore, each of these three syllogisms is invalid for another reason: The major term—canines, people who are dissatisfied with the government, human—must appear as the predicate of the conclusion. In the above syllogisms, it doesn't.

There is still another reason for the invalidity of the previous three syllogisms. In order for a syllogism to be valid, the middle term must be distributed at least once. Remember, the middle term is the one that appears in each of the two premises but does not appear in the conclusion. And remember that a term is distributed when every member of that class denoted by that term is being referred to.

In the first syllogism, the middle term *a canine* does not refer to *all* canines, merely to those occupied by dogs and to those occupied by wolves.

In the second syllogism, the middle term *people dissatisfied with the government* does not refer to all people dissatisfied with the government, merely to those occupied by anarchists and to those occupied by Harry.

In the third syllogism, the middle term *human* does not refer to all human beings, merely to those human beings represented by anarchists and to those represented by Harry.

The technical name for the error in reasoning that we have been describing is the **fallacy of the undistributed middle term.**

The last of the important rules in evaluating syllogisms is this: if a term is distributed in the conclusion, it must also be distributed in one of the premises. Note the following two syllogisms, both of which seem to have the same form:

A	B
All bank robbers are criminals.	All bank robbers are criminals.
Chris is not a criminal.	Chris is not a bank robber.
Therefore, Chris is not a bank robber.	Therefore, Chris is not a criminal.

In syllogism A, *Chris* is distributed in the conclusion and in the

second statement. *Bank robber* is distributed in the conclusion—
because Chris is excluded from the *whole* race of bank robbers—and
in the first statement—because the first statement talks about *all*
bank robbers.

In syllogism *B,* however, while *Chris* is distributed in the conclusion and in one of the premises, the same cannot be said for
criminals. Criminals is distributed in the conclusion—since Chris is
excluded from the *whole* race of criminals—but not in the first statement—since the first statement says nothing about all criminals,
merely those criminals occupied by bank robbers. Thus the syllogism is invalid. The following diagrams will clarify the invalidity:

Syllogism A: If Chris is excluded from the race of criminals and if the race of criminals includes bank robbers, then
Chris is automatically excluded from the race of bank robbers.

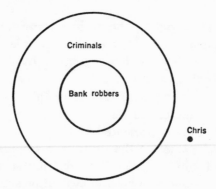

Syllogism B: If Chris is excluded from the race of bank
robbers, he is not necessarily excluded from the race of
criminals. He may be a criminal but not a bank robber, or
he may be a noncriminal.

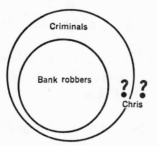

All we know is that Chris
does not occupy the circle
occupied by bank robbers.

Substituting the word *human* for the major term will clarify even further why syllogism B is invalid:

> All bank robbers are human.
> Chris is not a bank robber.
> Therefore, Chris is not human.

The fallacy that we have just been describing is known as the **fallacy of illicit distribution.**

Now let's summarize the techniques we can use to evaluate the form of a syllogism. First of all, we can diagram the syllogism by using points and circles to represent the terms of the syllogism. A circle will represent a class or a subclass and a point will represent a specific. This method is fine if we have a sheet of paper in front of us. We will be able to visualize what we can deduce from a pair of statements. However, we have to be careful to follow the statements very carefully. For instance,

> All craftsmen are meticulous.
> Some Russians are not meticulous.

First of all, we draw a circle that will comprise all meticulous persons. Then, since all craftsmen are meticulous, we put another circle inside the first one to represent all craftsmen. Now, the second statement says nothing about Russians who are meticulous; it merely says something about Russians who are not meticulous. Since *some* means *at least one,* the statement really means: "At least one Russian is not meticulous." Therefore, we must put the third circle outside the class of meticulous persons:

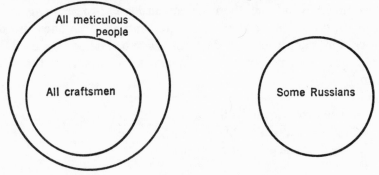

We can now conclude that some Russians are not craftsmen.

No Russians are Scandinavians
Some Scandinavians are blond.

We start by drawing two separate circles to represent Russians and Scandinavians. The second statement merely says that some of those Scandinavians are blond. Therefore the third circle will only partly overlap the circle of Scandinavians:

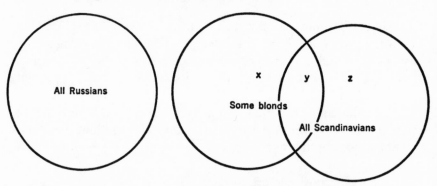

From these circles, we can see that the only conclusion is that some blondes are not Russian. The area occupied by x represents some blondes who are not Scandinavians; the area occupied by y represents those people who are both blond and Scandinavian; the area occupied by z represents those Scandinavians who are not blond.

The second way to test a syllogism is to substitute one term for another making sure that the statements are true ones. The principle here is that the form of a syllogism is valid for whatever terms appear in that syllogism. Hence, if the statements are true ones and the form is a valid one, then the conclusion has to be a true statement. If, on the other hand, the statements are true ones and the conclusion is not true, then the form has to be invalid. We used this technique when we substituted *human* for *criminals* in the syllogism:

All bank robbers are criminals.
Chris is not a bank robber.
Therefore, Chris is not a criminal.

Once we substituted *human,* we saw clearly that the conclusion *Therefore, Chris is not human* is absurd. Therefore, we could immediately recognize that the form of the syllogism was faulty, or invalid. Therefore, we can say that any syllogism with the form:

All X is Y.
Z is not X.
Therefore, Z is not Y.

is invalid. The substitution technique is not foolproof, but it offers perhaps the most vivid way to illustrate that a syllogism is invalid.

The third technique is to refer to the rules. It is important to realize that these rules are not arbitrary ones. Rather, they were formulated by analyzing every possible combination of terms within a syllogism and determining what common reasons were responsible for true statements yielding a false conclusion. The rules, consequently, are foolproof. Any syllogism that violates one of the rules will be an invalid one.

If you want to use the rules to check the validity of a syllogism, ask yourself the following questions. If your answer to any of the following questions is no, then you have an invalid syllogism:

1. Are there three sentences and only three sentences?

2. Does the third sentence begin either explicitly or implicitly with the word *therefore?*

3. Are there three terms and only three terms?

4. Does the subject of the conclusion appear in one and only one of the first two statements? (i.e., the minor term)

5. Does the predicate of the conclusion appear in the other and only in the other of the first two statements? (i.e., the major term)

6. Is there a term that appears in the first statement and in the second statement but not in the conclusion? (i.e., the middle term)

7. Does the middle term say something about all the members

of the class that belong to that term in at least one of the first two statements? (i.e., Is the middle term distributed at least once?)

Another way of phrasing this question is, If the statements are affirmative ones, is there the following relationship among the three terms: class—subclass—member of subclass? (i.e., is there a *true* middle?)

8. If the word *some* begins one of the first two statements, does the word *some* also begin the conclusion?

9. If there is a negative in the conclusion, is there also a negative in one of the first two statements?

10. Does at least one of the first two statements not begin with *some?*

11. Does at least one of the first two statements not contain a negative?

12. If a term is distributed in the conclusion, is it also distributed in one of the first two statements? In other words, if a term says something about each and every member in the conclusion, does it also say something about each and every member in one of the first two statements?

The final test for the validity of a syllogism is merely to consult the following list of valid forms. (This method is fine as long as this book is available.) Although there are over 250 different ways to set up syllogisms, only 24 of these are valid, and of those 24, only 15 are important.

Class I: statements with ALL

1. All A is B.
   (All) C is A.
   Therefore, (all) C is B.

Class II: statements with ALL ... SOME

2. All A is B.
Some C is A.
Therefore, some C is B.

3. All A is B.
Some A is C.
Therefore, some C is B.

4. All A is B.
Some C is A.
Therefore, some B is C.

5. All A is B.
Some A is C.
Therefore, some B is C.

Class III: statements with ALL . . . NO

6. All A is B.
No C is B.
Therefore, no C is A.
or, C is not A.

7. All A is B.
No B is C.
Therefore, no C is A.
or, C is not A.

8. All A is B.
No C is B.
Therefore, no A is C.
or, A is not C.

9. All A is B.
No B is C.
Therefore, no A is C.
or, A is not C.

Class IV: statements with ALL . . . SOME . . . NOT

10. All A is B.
Some A is not C.
Therefore, some B is
not C.

11. All A is B.
Some C is not B.
Therefore, some C is
not A.

Class V: statements with NO . . . SOME

12. No A is B.
Some A is C.
Therefore, some C is
not B.

13. No A is B.
Some C is A.
Therefore, some C is
not B.

14. No A is B.
Some B is C.
Therefore, some C is
not A.

15. No A is B,
Some C is B.
Therefore, some C is
not A.

Any true statements that are plugged into any of these fifteen patterns must yield a conclusion that is also true. For instance, let us look at the following two statements:

No anarchists are happy with the status quo.
Some people happy with the status quo are conservative.

The pattern here conforms to pattern *14:*

No A is B.
Some B is C.

The conclusion must be:

Some C is not A: "Therefore, some conservatives are not anarchists."

Another example:

No anarchists are happy with the status quo.
Tom is an anarchist.

These statements clearly fall into Class III, but they do not seem to conform to any of the four patterns cited in that class. However, by merely reversing the order of the two statements, we can easily identify with pattern *7* or pattern *9:*

Tom is an anarchist.	(All) A is B.
No anarchists are happy with the status quo.	No B is C.

The conclusion, therefore, is either:

People happy with the status quo are not (= do not include) Tom.	C is not A.
or	
Tom is not happy with the status quo.	A is not C.

We can regard this example in still another way:

All anarchists are not happy with the status quo.	All A is B.

Tom is an anarchist. (All) C is A.

Since we are clearly dealing with pattern *1*, the conclusion is:
Tom is not happy with the status quo. (All) C is B.

Now, this study of the syllogism may sound like a big fuss over nothing. After all, we don't talk in syllogisms, and it would be dreadfully boring if we did. The syllogism, however, is the most valuable tool we have in trying to determine the truth. It forces us to spell out exactly what we mean. It leaves nothing to inference. It demands that we be absolutely precise and clear. It forces us to distinguish between evidence and conclusions, to articulate exactly what that evidence is, and to examine the relationship between the evidence and the conclusion. In requiring us to articulate our premises, it allows us to distinguish between statements of fact and statements of opinion. The syllogism forces us to determine whether we are dealing with matters of truth or with matters of reasoning. In other words, if we disagree with a conclusion, the syllogism allows us immediately to determine whether we disagree with the conclusion because we disagree with one (or more) of the premises upon which that conclusion is based or because there has been some flaw in the way those premises have been used. When used cleanly, the syllogism strips away unnecessary verbiage, verbiage that can camouflage fallacies, and it exposes the fallacy logically and objectively.

Interlude: Human Nature

Know then thyself, presume not God to scan,
The proper study of mankind is man.
Placed on this isthmus of a middle state,
A being darkly wise, and rudely great:
With too much knowledge for the sceptic side,
With too much weakness for the stoic's pride,
He hangs between; in doubt to act, or rest;
In doubt to deem himself a god, or beast;
In doubt his mind or body to prefer;
Born but to die, and reasoning but to err;
Alike in ignorance, his reason such,
Whether he thinks too little, or too much:
Chaos of thought and passion, all confused;
Still by himself abused, or disabused;
Created half to rise, and half to fall;
Great lord of all things, yet a prey to all;
Sole judge of truth, in endless error hurled:
The glory, jest, and riddle of the world!

Pope, *An Essay on Man*, II, 1-18

The poles defined by Pope in the above verses make good sense. Human beings are indeed a bundle of contradictions. Endowed with reason, they will quickly put reason aside even while proclaiming they are being most reasonable: "Chaos of thought and passion, all confused."

Here are a few desultory comments upon human nature . . . no spectacular pronouncements; just a few casual observations.

First, most of us tend to think highly of people who agree with us or who share our positions on issues we feel are important. "We hardly find any persons of good sense except those who agree with us," says a maxim of La Rochefoucauld. Even people for whom we have little regard miraculously become elevated when we realize that their feelings complement our own.

Similarly, suppose I have neutral feelings toward a person. If you and I become close friends and if you dislike that person, chances are good that I too will begin to dislike that person. It is difficult to remain neutral in the face of a strong counter-emotion. Even though there may be no change in the relationship between that person and me, I, influenced by your feelings, will probably begin to see—or think I see—unattractive qualities in that person.

Indeed, we tend to adjust our beliefs and attitudes to our circumstances. We tend to believe what we want to believe. A young married couple, struggling to find an apartment and finally finding one that they would ordinarily consider an eyesore, will convince themselves that the place is really not all that bad, that it has charm, is quaint, perhaps is even cute, and that it will be quite nice after a bit of cosmetic work. But if they should then come upon a much nicer apartment, they will express relief and will comment on how awful the first place was.

We sometimes have a bizarre sense of what is just and unjust, fair and unfair, acceptable and unacceptable. A person desperately in need of a job will say, "I'll take anything." And indeed he will take anything. But after getting the job, he will soon forget those feelings and find the job unsatisfactory. A person gets a job at a certain salary, a salary that he thinks is fair and perhaps even generous ... until he finds out that a fellow worker is getting more; then that salary appears unfair and unsatisfactory. A person dreading a certain social event is indignant when he is not invited to that event; if he had been invited, he might not have gone; if he had gone, he would have done so reluctantly; regardless, he is outraged when there is no invitation. In a certain organization of five officials, four find that their offices have been bugged; the fifth, instead of feeling relieved that his privacy was not invaded, resents the fact that he was left out.

It is easy to let our imagination run away with us and to see dimensions to a situation that do not exist. Recall that classic scene in the Marx Brothers' "Duck Soup": throughout the movie, considerable animosity has existed between Groucho and Ambassador Trentino; Mrs. Teasdale, however, has been a peacemaker. In order to prevent war, she has talked with Trentino and has gotten him to meet with Groucho so that the two can reconcile themselves. Groucho replies:

> Mrs. Teasdale, you did a noble deed. I'd be unworthy of the high trust that's been placed in me if I didn't do everything within my power to keep our beloved Fredonia at peace with the world. I'd be only too happy to meet Ambassador Trentino and offer him on behalf of my country the right hand of good fellowship. And I feel sure that he will accept this gesture in the spirit in which it is offered. But suppose he doesn't. A fine thing that will be. I hold out my hand, and he refuses to accept it. That will add a lot to my prestige, won't it! Me, the head of a country snubbed by a foreign ambassador. Who does he think he is that he can come here and make a sap out of me in front of all my people. Think of it, I hold out my hand and that hyena refuses to accept it. Why, the cheap swine, he'll never get away with it.

Trentino enters at this point. "So, you refuse to shake hands with me!" Groucho retorts, and slaps Trentino. War is instantly declared.

Mark Twain in his *Mysterious Stranger* (Chapter 9) identifies what he considered "that large defect" in the human race: "the individual's distrust of his neighbor and his desire, for safety's or comfort's sake, to stand well in his neighbor's eye." These are perhaps harsh words, but they do illustrate that "glory, jest, and riddle of the world."

Final Words

*It is comforting to occupy the stable and well for-
tified positions erected by the learning of wise men
while the people down below you are wandering in
all directions and trying to find some path of life,
vying for reputation, fighting for prestige, striving
day and night to get power and to emerge on top.*

Lucretius, II, 7-13

Perhaps the most important principles to be gleaned from the pre-
ceding chapters are the following:

a. Be alert to anyone who speaks in absolutes: who uses words
such as *all, none, no one, never, always, everyone, must, immediately,* or who refers to a group of people as if all the members
have identical characteristics, beliefs, or attitudes.

b. Be alert to generalizations, especially to generalizations that
are not supported or that are supported from just one or two specific, unusual, or extreme examples.

c. Be alert to anyone who uses emotional language and evaluative words instead of objective, factual responses.

d. Do not confuse opinion, attitude, personal bias, speculation,
personal assurance, unsupported generalization with hard, factual
evidence.

e. Be sure that the issue under discussion is clear and precise, that its ramifications and complexities have been identified, that its goals have been identified, and that the words and concepts have been defined.

f. Be sure that the evidence is relevant to the specific topic of discussion, not to some related topic.

g. When an authority is referred to, do not automatically accept that authority unless his/its credentials are relevant to the issue under discussion.

h. Make sure that the conclusion follows from the evidence.

i. Be sure that you do not put others in a position where they have to make inferences and that you are not put in a position where you have to make inferences. In other words, be sure that necessary steps are not omitted in argument. Avoid making assumptions.

j. Wherever possible, do not allow rational discussions to become heated arguments. When a discussion becomes heated, stop the discussion, determine the source of the problem, clarify any misunderstandings, and then bring the discussion back to the topic. When people are disagreeing, make sure that they know the specific nature of their disagreement.

k. Make sure that the evidence is thorough, not selective.

l. Don't quibble; don't argue just for the sake of arguing.

m. Think critically. Never let a fallacy go by without making a mental note of it; even if you don't say anything, say to yourself, 'This is nonsense.'

n. Whenever you hear an argument, examine it before you accept its conclusions. Ask three questions:
1. Are the statements—the premises—the points being made and used as evidence—true?

2. Is the evidence complete? or has the evidence been one-sided?

3. Does the conclusion come incontrovertibly from the evidence? Or might a different conclusion just as easily have come from the evidence?

o. Finally, no matter how skilled in argument you may become, never forget the opening sentence of Poe's 'The Cask of Amontillado':

The thousand injuries of Fortunato I had borne as best I could, but when he ventured upon insult, I vowed revenge.

The world does not need another smart aleck.

Summary of Fallacies and Nonsense

Slogans
Transfer
Testimonial
Plain folks
Snob appeal
Statistics without context
Large numbers
Manufactured problem/ bad guy/ scapegoat
Arrant distortion/ card-stacking
The Command

Chapter 6: Suggestion

The hint
Accent
Selection
Tone of voice
Phraseology
Word choice and evaluative words
Metaphor
Juxtaposition
Irrelevant detail
Image words
Jargonese/ doublespeak/ gobbledygook
Controlling question

Chapter 8: Irrelevance

Ad hominem argument:
    abusive
    circumstantial
    guilt by association
    poisoning the well
Passing the buck: *tu quoque*/shifting the blame
    counter-question
Irrelevant reason
Non sequitur
Irrelevant detail
Appeal to force *(argumentum ad baculum)*
Appeal to ignorance *(argumentum ad ignorantiam)*
Appeal to authority *(argumentum ad verecundiam)*:

Ipse dixit (He said it)
    Appeal to the past or to past authority
    Vague authority
    Apriority
    Appeal to faith
    The sacred cow
    Aphorisms, clichés, slogans, proverbs, platitudes
    Jargon
    Appeal to tradition or precedent
    Abuse of etymology
Appeal to numbers:
    Using mean instead of mode
    Misleading percentages
    Misleading sampling techniques: limited sample
                                              small sample
    Vague statistics
        Misleading statistics
        Appeal to large numbers
Confident speculation:
    Personal assurance
    Personal experience
    Domino theory
    Omniscience
    Confusion of speculation with fact

Chapter 9: Diversion

The red herring:
    Use of humor, sarcasm, parody, innuendo, ridicule, bodily gesture
    Witty remark
    Literal interpretation of figurative remark
    Intimidation
    Petty objection/ nit-picking
    Feigning ignorance

The straw man:
    Extension of ideas
    Putting words in opponent's mouth
    Attacking the example
    Attacking the alternative
    Shifting to another problem

Chapter 11: Ambiguity and Inference

Verbal ambiguity
Ambiguity of statement
Ambiguity of tone
Irony
Accent
Quoting out of context
Quoting selectively
Damnation by faint praise
Amphiboly
Grammatical ambiguity
Juxtaposition
Enthymemes

Chapter 12: Confusion and Inference

Verbal confusion
Equivocation
Fustianism
Double standards/ doublethink
Limited perspective
Circular reasoning/ begging the question
Confusing complement with opposite
Composition
Division
Addition
Definition because of common characteristics
Confusing opinion, speculation, inference with fact
All-some/ most-one

Chapter 13: Cause and Effect

Confusing contributory, sufficient, and necessary causes
Confusing remote cause with immediate cause
Rationalization
Reversal of cause and effect
The *post hoc* fallacy
Inferring that simultaneous occurrences necessarily have a cause and effect relationship

Procrastination
One step at a time
Too many *ifs*
Domino theory
Red herring
Changing the words
Arguments of tradition and precedent
Rephrasing the question

Chapter 20: *Some semantic problems*

Verbal ambiguity
Syntactic ambiguity (amphiboly)
Since
As
And
Both ... not
All ... not
Or
Assuming that an alternative is false because the other alternative is true
If
Fallacy of affirming the consequent
Fallacy of denying the antecedent
Abuse of chain (serial/hypothetical) conditions
The
Be

Bibliography

All the following titles are enthusiastically recommended, and each has influenced the preparation of this book in one way or another.

Baum, Robert, *Logic*, New York: Holt, Rinehart and Winston, Inc., 1975.

Baker, Samm Sinclair, *The Permissible Lie*, Boston: Beacon Press, 1968. An intriguing study of half-truth, trickery, and strategy in advertising.

Beardsley, Monroe C., *Practical Logic*, Englewood Cliffs, N.J.: Prentice-Hall, Inc. 1950. A fine introduction to the principles of logic. There is much more here than most readers will want to use, but whatever chapter the reader turns to he will find clear and thorough.

————, *Thinking Straight*, 4th ed., Englewood Cliffs, N.J.: Prentice-Hall, Inc., 1975. A more compact version of the title just cited. The explanations are sometimes surprisingly prolix, but the examples are excellent.

Bentham, Jeremy, *Bentham's Handbook of Political Fallacies*, edited by Harold Larrabee, New York: Thomas Y. Crowell Company, Apollo Edition, 1971. A fine edition. Larrabee explains many of Bentham's allusions.

Brown, J. A. C., *Techniques of Persuasion*, Baltimore: Penguin Books, 1963. Sometimes technical but highly readable and thorough.

Campbell, Stephen K., *Flaws and Fallacies in Statistical Thinking*, Englewood Cliffs, N.J.: Prentice-Hall, Inc., 1974.

Chase, Stuart, *Guides to Straight Thinking*, New York: Harper & Row, 1956.

Copi, Irving M., *Introduction to Logic*, 4th ed., New York: Macmillan Publishing Co., Inc., 1972. A standard text, but not always very readable.

Corbett, Edward J., *Classical Rhetoric*, New York: Oxford University Press, 1965. Chapter II, "Discovery of Arguments," is particularly good.

Eisenberg, Abne M. and Joseph A. Ilardo, *Argument: An Alternative to Violence,* Englewood Cliffs, N.J.: Prentice-Hall, Inc., 1972. Rarely does one find a book with so much common sense per page.

Fearnside, W. Ward and William B. Holther, *Fallacy: The Counterfeit of Argument,* Englewood Cliffs, N.J.: Prentice-Hall, Inc., Spectrum Book, 1959. The authors itemize fifty-one types of fallacies, present examples, and offer rebuttals.

Fischer, David Hackett, *Historians' Fallacies,* New York: Harper & Row, 1970. Probably the most thorough collection of types of fallacies in this bibliography. Heavy reading at times but worth the effort.

Freeley, Austin J., *Argumentation and Debate: Rational Decision Making,* Belmont, California: Wadsworth Publishing Company, Inc., 1976.

Hayakawa, S.I., *Language in Thought and Action,* 3rd ed., New York: Harcourt Brace Jovanovich, Inc., 1972.

Herzog, Arthur, *The B.S. Factor,* Baltimore: Penguin Books, Inc., 1974. Idiosyncratic and amusing. The subtitle reads: "The theory and technique of faking it in America." Herzog's B.S. factors are faithful to that subtitle.

"How to Detect Propaganda," from *Propaganda Analysis,* November, 1937, The Institute for Propaganda Analysis, Inc. Reprinted in *Modern Rhetoric* by Cleanth Brooks and Robert Penn Warren, New York: Harcourt, Brace and Company, 1949.

Huff, Darrell, *How to Lie with Statistics,* New York: W.W. Norton & Company, Inc., 1954. By now one of the classics.

Kahane, Howard, *Logic and Contemporary Rhetoric,* 2nd ed., Belmont, California: Wadsworth Publishing Company, Inc., 1976. A very good introduction to the principles of clear thinking and to the avoidance of gullibility. The copious examples are excellent.

Manicas, Peter T., and Arthur N. Kruger, *Logic: The Essentials,* New York: McGraw-Hill Book Company, 1976. Probably the most technical book in this bibliography. The material, however, is presented with clarity.

Michalos, Alex C., *Improving Your Reasoning,* Englewood Cliffs, N.J.: Prentice-Hall, Inc., 1970. Michalos presents about a hundred types of fallacies and illustrates them. The illustrations sometimes fall short, but the categories are important ones.

Parkinson, C. Northcote, *Parkinson's Law,* New York: Ballantine Books, 1971.

Peter, Laurence J. and Raymond Hull, *The Peter Principle,* New York: William Morrow and Company, Inc., 1969.

Ruby, Lionel and Robert E. Yarber, *The Art of Making Sense,* 3rd ed., New York: J. B. Lippincott Company, 1974.

Thouless, Robert H., *Straight and Crooked Thinking,* London: The English

Universities Press Ltd., 1953. Simon and Schuster now publishes it under the title *How to Think Straight.* This is an absolutely splendid and witty little book that is completely faithful to its original title. It goes into the many tricks of the trade and tells you what to do if the tricks are used upon you.

Weinland, James D., *How to Think Straight,* Totowa, New Jersey: Little-field, Adams & Co., 1963.

Willis, Hulon, *Logic, Language, and Composition,* Cambridge, Mass.: Winthrop Publishers, Inc., 1975. An ingenious book that inter-sperses chapters on logic with chapters on principles of grammar, punctuation, spelling, writing, and style. The chapters on logic are not a major portion of the book, but what Willis does present, he presents well.

Ziegelmueller, George W. and Charles A. Dause, *Argumentation: Inquiry and Advocacy,* Englewood Cliffs, N.J.: Prentice-Hall, Inc., 1975. One of the most valuable books in this bibliography.

Ancillary Sources

Beiser, Arthur, *The Mainstream of Physics,* Reading, Mass.: Addison-Wes-ley Publishing Company, Inc., 1962.

Bailey, Thomas A., *The American Pageant,* 4th ed., Lexington, Mass.: D. C. Heath and Company, 1971.

Hoyt's New Cyclopedia of Practical Quotations, New York: Funk & Wag-nalls Company, 1927.

Hurd, Charles, *A Treasury of Great American Speeches,* New York: Haw-thorn Books, Inc., 1959.

The Oxford Dictionary of Quotations, London: Oxford University Press, 1941.

Index